NATURAL
ABUNDANCE

OTHER TITLES IN THE

LIBRARY OF
HIDDEN KNOWLEDGE

The New Master Key System

The New Science of Getting Rich

NATURAL
ABUNDANCE

Ralph Waldo Emerson's Guide to Prosperity

EDITED BY RUTH L. MILLER

LIBRARY OF
HIDDEN KNOWLEDGE

ATRIA BOOKS
New York London Toronto Sydney

BEYOND WORDS
Hillsboro, Oregon

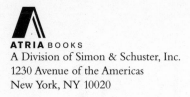

ATRIA BOOKS
A Division of Simon & Schuster, Inc.
1230 Avenue of the Americas
New York, NY 10020

BEYOND WORDS
20827 N.W. Cornell Road, Suite 500
Hillsboro, Oregon 97124-9808
503-531-8700 / 503-531-8773 fax
www.beyondword.com

Managing editor: Lindsay S. Brown
Editor: Gretchen Stelter
Copyeditor: Jade Chan
Proofreader: Mark Antonides
Design: Devon Smith
Composition: William H. Brunson Typography Services

First Atria Books/Beyond Words hardcover edition March 2011

ATRIA BOOKS and colophon are trademarks of Simon & Schuster, Inc. Beyond Words Publishing is a division of Simon & Schuster, Inc.

For more information about special discounts for bulk purchases, please contact Simon & Schuster Special Sales at 1-866-506-1949 or business@simonandschuster.com.

The Simon & Schuster Speakers Bureau can bring authors to your live event. For more information or to book an event, contact the Simon & Schuster Speakers Bureau at 1-866-248-3049 or visit our website at www.simonspeakers.com.

Manufactured in the United States of America

10 9 8 7 6 5 4 3 2 1

Library of Congress Cataloging-in-Publication Data

　Natural abundance : Ralph Waldo Emerson's guide to prosperity / edited by Ruth L. Miller.
　　　p.　cm.
　Includes bibliographical references.
　　1. Wealth.　2. Self-reliance.　3. Emerson, Ralph Waldo, 1803–1882.
　I. Miller, Ruth L.
　HB251.N38　2011
　332.024—dc22
　　　　　　　　　　　　　　　　　　　　　　　　　　2010042454

ISBN: 978-1-58270-285-8
ISBN: 978-1-4516-1300-1 (ebook)

The corporate mission of Beyond Words Publishing, Inc.: *Inspire to Integrity*

To once and future generations of seekers after the Good Life.

Man was born to be rich, or inevitably grows rich by the use of his faculties; by the union of thought with nature.

FROM EMERSON'S LECTURE "WEALTH, THE CONDUCT OF LIFE" (1860)

CONTENTS

NOTE FROM THE PUBLISHER

The Library of Hidden Knowledge grew from the inspiration to preserve and revitalize original works of spiritual thought, philosophy, and esoteric writings at least seventy-five years old that are either out of print, difficult to find, forgotten, or missing from the bookshelves of many of our neighborhood bookstores and public libraries.

The first two books in the series are *The New Science of Getting Rich*, from the original work by Wallace D. Wattles, and *The New Master Key System*, based on the writings of Charles F. Haanel. Both books along with *Natural Abundance* were edited by Ruth L. Miller, a scholar who understands the power and significance of these works and the need to reveal them to new generations of readers in the twenty-first century and beyond.

In the Library of Hidden Knowledge, you are invited to discover these sources of inspiration for many of our modern-day spiritual teachers and leaders. We offer you the opportunity to read the original texts along with the modern scholarly interpretations that bring new life and understanding to the content.

Ralph Waldo Emerson inspired the movement and philosophy known as Transcendentalism, which has left a deep imprint on American spiritual thought and continues to influence generations of truth-seekers around the world. It is my pleasure and honor to present *Natural Abundance* as the third book in the series.

The Library of Hidden Knowledge will continue to expand and will include other contemporary scholars' interpretations of timeless works that should live on and not be forgotten. We invite you to collect them all and treasure these precious pearls of wisdom.

Enjoy,

Cynthia Black

Cynthia Black
Editor in Chief

PREFACE

The book you have before you is the third in a series called the Library of Hidden Knowledge. For this series I've taken powerful gems of wisdom written in the late nineteenth and early twentieth centuries and "translated" them into language and formats that are more comfortable for modern readers. This one, however, is different from the others. Wallace D. Wattles, who wrote *The Science of Getting Rich*, and Charles Haanel, author of *The Master Key System*, had written guidebooks for people seeking a path to prosperity. Ralph Waldo Emerson, on the other hand, deliberately hid his guidelines for action so that only "those with eyes to see and ears to hear" would find them.

I must admit I was somewhat hesitant to play with the words of a man whose works are considered some of the greatest in American literature, but the idea had been growing on me for a while. I've long felt, as I did with all "my" authors (Emma Curtis Hopkins and Emilie Cady, as well as Wallace Wattles and Charles Haanel), that it was a shame that so many modern readers have been prevented from experiencing the riches Emerson had to offer by the complex language and lack of structure in his essays. And as Nature will always provide what we need, over the past few years relative strangers have given me not one but two complete works of Emerson, as if to encourage the effort. Then, of course, my publisher asked for a new project for this series. What more push could Nature give?

So I took on the project. The first step was to select those essays that seemed to most directly address living an abundant life. Like most Americans, I'd read several of Emerson's essays in school—in high school English class, in college American literature classes, and in seminary. I'd even taught a few of them to seminary students and delivered a few sermons based on them, so I felt that I knew enough to select the most relevant ones. Sadly, that meant leaving out a couple of my favorites ("History" and "Circles"), but they didn't really address the topic at hand.

Once I'd chosen the relevant pieces, I needed to interpret them. Now, Emerson didn't write essays in the usual sense of the term. His published writings are more like collections of comments from his journals and lecture notes—a sequence of carefully crafted sentences and paragraphs, without a beginning, middle, or end to the piece. There are no opening overviews and no closing summaries—not even a line of logic or reasoning—but simply a stream of thoughts and ideas regarding the topic at hand.

So the first step was translating his ideas line by line, merely to find modern ways to express the most important and relevant ideas. In the process, I was amazed and delighted. Virtually every paragraph had glowing gems of metaphysical wisdom. Every essay brought a deeper understanding of how to allow Nature's processes to support our fulfillment.

Then I worked through my initial interpretation, no longer simply following Emerson's stream of thought but removing what would not be meaningful to a modern reader and highlighting the critical ideas, organizing the material by subject headings, and calling out essential points.

The more I worked with his writings, the more I appreciated what Emerson understood about who we are and what we can be. The closer I got to his essential thoughts, the more powerful I found them to be. Essentially he tells us that Nature works in such a way that when we stop listening to others and begin to follow our inner guidance, thinking and acting as our true selves, a higher wisdom working outside space and time ensures our fulfillment. He goes on to say that conformity and consistency get in our way, but because we always receive what we give, expressing our unique gifts moves us off the wheel of chance and into a life of greatness and abundant satisfaction.

This was exciting stuff! But his ideas needed opportunities for readers to practice them. So I've included summary points and exercises, putting together the kind of guide that would be most useful to people seeking a more abundant life in today's world.

Doing this project has become a joyful process of discovery and delight, especially once I got over my awe of the great man and his language. It's my hope that, as with the other works in this series, my "updated" version will not only give you, the reader, the benefit of Emerson's powerful ideas, but also make it easier for you to make sense of his original works, some of which have been included in the second half of this volume.

Getting the Most from This Book

While Emerson didn't try to help his readers or listeners apply his ideas, this book has been designed to make both understanding and practicing Emerson's ideas easier. It's divided into two sections, the first containing my interpretations followed by Emerson's original essays.

At the beginning of each interpretation, I've written a brief overview of that particular essay.

The Essential Points at the end of each of my interpretations are a kind of summary and may also serve as affirmations or guides for readers to take with them in daily life.

The suggested exercises called Applying the Principles are based on the kinds of exercises that are used in the many study groups, centers, and churches that have grown up around these ideas. I've worked through and taught all the recommended exercises numerous times over a couple of decades and can attest to their effectiveness in accomplishing the change of consciousness that Emerson encourages.

You'll achieve the best results if you start a journal or notebook while you're going through this book, for notes and questions on the text and for doing the exercises. I recommend reading the whole first part through once, spending some time exploring the second part, and then going back to the first part, reading one chapter at a time and working through the exercises (at least starting the ones that take several days or weeks) before moving on to the next chapter.

Blessings on your journey!

ACKNOWLEDGMENTS

Many thanks to all the folks at Beyond Words for being willing to consider this project, taking it on, and making it the best product it can be—especially Cindy Black for her vision and constancy, Dan Frost for his gentle guidance and good humor, and to Gretchen Stelter and Lindsay S. Brown for their thoughtful editing and queries. Well done all!

INTRODUCTION

Ralph Waldo Emerson transcended the limitations of the religious and social norms of his day. Using common sense, a love of nature, and his own particular genius, he expressed a higher truth about who we are and how the world gives us exactly what we demand from it. In the process, he became the first great American philosopher and a wealthy man.

Born in Massachusetts in 1803, Emerson was among the first generation of citizens to be born in the newly formed United States of America. Following in his father's footsteps, he was trained as a Unitarian/Congregationalist minister at Harvard Divinity School. There he became familiar with the ancient origins of Western literature and science. He also came to understand that what the clergy preached in the churches was not the same as what the theologians were discovering and teaching in the seminaries.

Called to minister in Boston, Emerson worked diligently to open the minds of his congregants. Then one Easter, as the story goes, he decided to eliminate the traditional Communion service on the grounds that Unitarians did not worship Jesus as a god, but rather honored him as an elder brother, prophet, and master teacher of the one God's laws. The board sent him home to consider whether he truly wanted to be a minister in that church. He did not return.

Instead, he went to Europe to see the great historical sites and to meet some of the writers who were influencing his thinking.

He returned to the United States in 1836 with the conviction that he could make a living as a writer-lecturer and proceeded to write his first essay, "Nature." It took him weeks of painstaking effort to put just the right words and just the right sentences in just the right places in his long, complicated paragraphs. But it paid off. His first work took the nation by storm. Newspaper editors, critics, and college professors were delighted with this distinctly American approach to philosophy—and they wanted more. In a few years he went from being an obscure, out-of-work minister to being the voice of the country, traveling and speaking and writing all across the continent.[1,2]

Soon a movement grew up around him. Writers and poets living in and around his hometown of Concord, Massachusetts, joined him for long dinners, with longer conversations following. Emerson lived near the edge of town, about a mile from the town square. His was one of the larger houses, with a fine library, acreage, a farmyard, and a pond called Walden hidden in a small forest. One neighbor, a young man named Henry David Thoreau, built a small cabin alongside that pond and wrote a book of his own, destined to become a classic: *Walden*. Another neighbor had several daughters, one of whom listened carefully to those long conversations and went on to write many books herself; she was Louisa May, the daughter of Emerson's great friend Bronson Alcott. In fact, Emerson was the model for the rich neighbor with the wonderful library in her classic *Little Women*.

People of all walks of life would go to great lengths to hear the popular Mr. Emerson. At Wednesday evening talks in Concord, at

Chautauqua presentations, or on the "lecture circuit" around the country, farmers and their families would sit next to lawyers, doctors, and college professors, typically responding to Emerson's comments with something like "I can't understand a word he says, but I feel so good when I hear him say it." After a while it wasn't even necessary for him to speak; in the final years of his life, when his mind was no longer functioning, simply seeing him sit on the dais with other speakers satisfied the audience.

Yet perhaps because he was so popular and because so much of what was popularized focused only on the need to transcend materialism and reconnect with Nature and natural processes, some of his other core ideas were lost to future generations. They were there but buried in the long sentences and extended paragraphs of often overlooked essays. There they lay like hidden jewels, to be discovered only by the few who were willing to take the time to seek them out.

Among those who have found them are some of America's greatest healers and teachers. But like the works from which their ideas were drawn, few but their own students and followers know of these people.

Emma Curtis Hopkins was one. Credited with thousands of healings and teaching hundreds of healers and ministers from the 1880s to the 1920s, she knew Emerson's work inside and out, and integrated it with Eastern classics such as the *Tao Te Ching*, *Bhagavad Gita*, *Zend-Avesta*, and *Qur'an*. Her Chicago seminary taught Emerson's basic principles as truths to be found in all sacred traditions, emanating from the One-Mind that most of us call God and that Emerson called Nature or the Over-Soul.[3]

Charles and Myrtle Fillmore, who founded the Unity School of Christianity, were great fans of Emerson; in fact, that's how they came to know each other. They studied with Hopkins and went on to publish hundreds of books, along with the *Daily Word* magazine, and established the Silent Unity prayer ministry, which ends each session with one of Emerson's affirmations: "Wherever we are, God is, and all is well!"

Another of Emerson's followers was Ernest Holmes, Hopkins's last student and the founder of The Institute for Religious Science, from which thousands of United Centers for Spiritual Living have emerged all over the world. His book *The Science of Mind* is a classic in its own right.

Emmet Fox is another. A British immigrant and amazingly popular minister in New York City during the Depression, Fox wrote *The Sermon on the Mount* and *Diagrams for Living*, two books that are often still used as auxiliary texts in 12-step programs. He, too, credited Emerson with many of his early inspirations, as have thousands of other ministers, practitioners, and teachers around the world.

Even Gandhi and Martin Luther King, Jr., referred to Emerson as a major source of inspiration for their lives and work. These people found power in Emerson's writings and developed their own methods and processes to apply that power. They went on to teach thousands and transform the lives of millions.

Then at the turn of the twenty-first century, Rhonda Byrne was given a photocopy of Wattles's *The Science of Getting Rich* and discovered a way of thinking and acting that was, to her, entirely new. It saved her life and led to the amazingly popular video and book *The Secret*. Among the teachers she discovered who knew this secret and whom she quoted in *The Secret* is Ralph Waldo Emerson. Byrne, like many others before her, found gems of wisdom in what the great nineteenth-century philosopher offered that could still transform lives as they had for the past 160-plus years.

We, too, can find those gems if we're willing to look for them or, perhaps more accurately, have the eyes and patience to see them. This book is an attempt to make that a little easier by making those hidden jewels of wisdom more accessible to the modern, Internet-oriented, twenty-first-century reader. It's offered in the hopes that perhaps we, too, can experience the benefits of this great man's willingness to integrate his heart's knowing and his intellect's understanding.

If we do, perhaps we'll be led to transcend the ills of this time and culture, as he and his friends did in their time. Then we can also experience the deep, abiding peace of a truly abundant life.

Notes

1. A wonderful biography incorporating notes from many of Emerson's journals is *Emerson: The Mind on Fire*, by Robert D. Richardson, Jr. (Berkeley: University of California Press, 1995).
2. A delightful insight into his behavior may be found in *Mr. Emerson's Cook*, by Judith Byron Schachner (New York: Dutton Children's Books, 1998).
3. For a detailed biography of Emma Curtis Hopkins, see Gail Harley's *Emma Curtis Hopkins: Forgotten Founder of New Thought* (Syracuse, NY: Syracuse University Press, 2002). For an introduction to Hopkins's writings and life, see Ruth L. Miller's *Unveiling Your Hidden Power: Emma Hopkins' Metaphysics for the 21st Century* (Beaverton, OR: Wise Woman Press, 2006).

INTERPRETATIONS

MODERNIZED FOR
THE TWENTY-FIRST
CENTURY READER

Don't be too timid and squeamish about your actions.
All life is an experiment.
The more experiments you make the better.

I

ON NATURE'S RICHES, BEAUTY, AND LAWS

Emerson knew that being truly wealthy always includes experiencing great beauty, and that real, lasting wealth can only be acquired through understanding natural processes and working with them.

Finding True Wealth

If you know the delights to be found in the waters, the forests, and the heavens, and know how to experience their magic, you are truly rich. This is what all the parks, villas, gardens, and preserves of the wealthy aim for and yet so often fail to provide.

If only the rich were wealthy in the way the poor fantasize! The poor young person respects rich people because they have a fenced-in estate with a carefully designed landscape. The rich live in large, designer-furnished homes and socialize with celebrities. They travel in chartered jets and limousines to distant cities that youthful fantasy fills with romance. Young people, believing themselves to be poor, compare all these ideals to their own small homes and feel as if they are living in shacks, barely surviving.

But we don't need to live in mansions or go to Italy or Tahiti to find such glories. The beauty of the sky meeting the earth is in every landscape. The stars at night glow in any backyard with the same spiritual glory that may be found in Egypt's deserts. Beauty breaks in everywhere; the clouds and colors of morning and evening can make any landscape magical. Each of us has the capacity to experience the riches that Nature offers, wherever we are.

Everywhere, there are days when the world reaches its perfection. It may happen in any season of the year, when the air, the sun and clouds, and the earth form a wonderful harmony. Everything that has life seems satisfied; even the cattle resting on the ground seem to have peaceful thoughts, and solitary places don't seem lonely. On such a day, at the edge of the forest, we remember ancient tales of forest magic, and the silent trees invite us to come live with them and leave our life of self-important trifles. On such a day, we could walk on into the opening landscape and let each new vista, each new discovery, fill our minds—until all memory of home and work is crowded out by the fullness of the present moment. These enchanted moments, available to all, are like medicine; they cleanse and heal us.

My house stands in the low land, with a limited view, but when I go with my friend to the shore of the little river that passes through our town and step into our boat, it takes just one stroke of the paddle to leave politics and personalities behind. We pass into a magical realm of sunset and moonlight, almost too bright to enter without spiritual preparation. We move into this incredible beauty; we dip our hands in this living painting; our eyes are bathed by these wondrous lights and forms. It's an instant, glorious holiday, a moment of deep enjoyment that lasts forever.

Here, in Nature's perfection, is a holiness that shames our religions, a reality that makes our civilized customs meaningless. Here, no history, no church, no state insists on our attention.

We come into our own true essence when we make friends with the natural world. Though our society teaches us to take it all for granted, we can never part with it; it's our true home. The rock and soil of this earth is, to our eyes, hands, and feet, like water is to our thirst—an old friend, dear and honest, refreshing us and reminding us of our true selves.

Nature Works for Us

It may seem frivolous to more practical people to spend this kind of time in Nature's beauty, but to those who complain of our paying attention to beauty rather than to the work to be done, I suggest they consider that our love of Nature is really what lifts us out of our poor humanness. For, sadly, humanity is fallen. In our dullness and selfishness, we look up to the wonders of Nature, rather than the natural world looking up to us. If our lives flowed with the energy that is our birthright, the flowing brook that we've admired would seem dull by comparison. For it glows only by reflected light, while the stream of living spirit that is available to us sparkles with the true fire of creation.

Still, understanding Nature's processes gives us the tools for creating our own good life. Through transformation on transformation, Nature's processes lead to the formation of the simplest particles and the most complex galaxies, with all their stars and planets. Nature gives us all forms of creatures.

Nature does all this with elegant simplicity, through the interaction of two principles. The first of these is Motion (energy, change, the tendency to move apart—the quantum wavicles called *fermions*), and the second is Rest (matter, form, or identity, the tendency to unite—the quantum wavicles called *bosons*). The whole code of natural law is written in these two fundamental principles.[1]

Nature is so elegant that just one substance (the fundamental quantum field) becomes all the variety of the universe. However complex a form may be—star, sand, fire, water, tree, humanity—it's still that one substance, showing up in some combination of energy and matter, motion and rest. It's all interconnected, too; even the most stylish model striding the runways of New York or Paris is directly related to the sea, the stars, and the Himalayan mountain chain, and has an animal aspect, rude as a bear's.

Nature is always consistent. As a result, we can predict, from any one object, all the parts and properties of any other. For those who are trained to see it, a bit of stone from a city wall proves that humanity must exist—and the city, too. Nature made the stone, the mason, and the house—all are part of her process—so that humanity can dwell in these cities.

The study of geology and astronomy has taught us to let go of our insignificant ideas of importance and accept Nature's immensities. Nature arms and equips an animal to find its place and live on earth and at the same time arms and equips another animal to destroy it. As we observe individual animals—for example, the cat toying with the mouse—the process may seem harsh and unforgiving, but seen from the perspective of boundless space and time, all of Nature's changes pass in awe-inspiring harmony and order, without violence or distress. Species and star systems emerge, evolve, explore, and are extinguished in a great dance of beauty and order.

If we look at Nature's work this way, we seem to catch a glimpse of a system in transition. The direction is always onward; Nature is always bringing materials from the past forward, in their most advanced stage, to form something new. It's a long way from granite to an oyster—and farther yet to Plato preaching the immortality of the soul—yet all must emerge as Nature unfolds her infinite variety. She keeps her laws and so transcends them.

Always More, Always Beyond

We are part of Nature's evolution, and we contribute to it. The process continues through every atom, through all the species, through history, and in the activities of each human being.

My toddler's day is one of Nature's most beautiful examples of development. Not yet able to rank or choose from the variety of experiences available to him, the little one is led by his senses and called by every sight and sound. Given a selection of interesting shapes, colors, textures, and noisemakers, he is delighted with every new thing, consumed by a near madness, until at night he's overpowered by fatigue and ends another day in peaceful slumber. Yet Nature has used this mania for her own purpose. She has worked every one of the child's abilities and encouraged his body's symmetrical growth, through all the positions and movements he's gotten into trying to reach whatever has caught his attention. The child is led by natural instincts to his own good, through a process so perfect that only Nature could conceive it.

We all live best in the same way. We don't eat to live; we eat because the meal tastes good and we're hungry. We choose what suits and delights us, and Nature uses our choices for our good and the good of all. And all the while, the universe expands, becoming more complex and more organized.

This expansion is built into every natural process. Nature sends no creature, no human being, into the world without adding a small excess to its basic qualities: a little shove to put it on its way, a slight generosity, a drop too much. No one is quite sane; each of us has a slight twist in our thinking. Without electricity in the atmosphere, the air would rot, and without excitement, we would be ineffective in our activity. Just as we aim above the mark to hit it, so Nature sends us onward a little wrongheadedly in the direction of our goals so we'll overshoot and accomplish them.

Plants demonstrate this same excess. They don't content themselves with throwing off a single seed but fill the air and earth with an abundance of seeds such that, if thousands perished, still thousands may plant themselves that hundreds may come up, that tens may reach maturity, and that one, at least, may replace the parent. All things express the same intentional abundance, which shows us that our own abundant supply is always assured.

Foolish Riches

Our experience in the natural world, though, is that promise always exceeds the performance. We live in a system of approximations where every completion points to some other possibility, which is also temporary. Nature leads us on and on, but somehow we never arrive. Our music, our poetry, and our language itself are not satisfactions but suggestions. Though we eat and drink our fill, still we hunger and thirst; we experience the literal meaning (as opposed to the usual understanding) of the Buddha's first Noble Truth: "no thing ever fully satisfies."[2]

The hunger for wealth fools the eager pursuer. What's the goal? Surely it's to have more experiences of beauty and comfort, safe from any distressing intrusions, but what a complex process to attain such a simple end! This palace of bricks and stone, these servants, these stocks and bonds, this international trade—all for a clear, high, and spiritual experience of beauty? No. As we've already seen, the experience of beauty is too easy to find. Instead, all these things come from repeated efforts to make life easier and to expand opportunities.

For most wealth seekers, having riches was good at first. It fed the body, delighted the senses, silenced the creaking door, and brought friends together in a warm and pleasant room. Sadly, though, in the effort to acquire these, the primary purpose is too often forgotten, and the means become the end. Now the wealth seeker has no room or time for truth, beauty, or good sense. In short, it was all for nothing. This is the foolishness of the rich.

Today the governments of the world are made up of these foolish rich, and the masses are not understood to be citizens but to be *poor people*—that is, people who wish they were rich. And the rich folk who make up the governments, having forgotten their own original goals, are like the sad fellow who has interrupted a conversation to make a speech and now has forgotten what he was going to say. To all appearances there is no real aim to the society, the government, or the nations. All have become slaves to the ever-changing little things, the details and particulars of the day. We have a hundred foolish expectations. We anticipate a new era from an election or invention, but the new era brings with it all the old issues. They say that everything will be produced and prepared faster and faster, but nothing is really gained. Nature's laws cannot be cheated. In such a world we can't help but wonder if true beauty and riches can ever be grasped.

True Wealth through Understanding

Humanity is more than a product and expression of Nature. While it sometimes seems that Nature is a vast promise, not easily explained, her secret untold because it is untellable, in truth, human beings hold within us the totality of Nature's being. Each of us carries the universe in our minds; all of astronomy, physics, biology, and chemistry exist in our thoughts. We can't even tie our shoes without recognizing laws that bind the farthest reaches of Nature: the moon, the planets, gas, crystals, geometry, and numbers. Every known fact in natural science was felt intuitively by someone before it was actually verified, and common sense is evident in even the most advanced experiments. This means that any of us can discover Nature's secrets.

If instead of *thinking* about Nature—identifying ourselves as a creation or product *outside* Nature—we allow ourselves to *feel* its soul running through us, then we find peace unfolding in our hearts and the unending wisdom of Nature's processes revealing themselves in our awareness. As the ancient Hindu texts and shamanic teachings from many cultures demonstrate, we can find within our own minds explanations of processes and structures in deep space and inside the cells of organisms that our sciences have only recently begun to be able to measure. Then we realize that the uneasiness we've been experiencing comes from looking too much at one aspect of Nature, namely Motion (energy and change). It's only by resting in the beauty of the natural world that we find the sanity and calm we need to expose and cure the insanity of most of our human activity.

This is because Nature's universal laws exist in our minds as ideals and appear around us as things and processes embodied in the world. This is why we're so affected by the beauty and complexity of natural objects. We're the same thought as they are, all in one interconnected form, without the artificial barriers of humanity's fabled "fall" into the appearance of isolated, separated individuals.

When human beings identify themselves as solid, separate beings, like ice crystals, we don't really speak to each other but to an impersonation—another imagined crystal. But the Power in us that knows the whole, that recognizes our oneness, is the same divine Power we see in the smile of morning and in every drop of rain. Every moment is a teacher, and divine Wisdom is infused into every form.

Essential Points

- Nature is always consistent. She keeps her laws and so transcends them. The direction is always onward.
- Each of us can experience all the riches that the world offers wherever we are. We choose what suits and delights us, and Nature uses our choices for our good and the good of all.
- The foolishness of the rich is that the primary purpose of wealth is forgotten; the means become the end, so there's no room or time for truth, beauty, or good sense.
- When we focus on Nature's Motion, we tend to get lost in the changing details and see ourselves as separate products of something greater than we are, and we somehow never fully grasp what we seek.
- When we *feel* Nature's beauty and harmony, we experience rest and begin to see that all of Nature—substance, laws, processes— is in each and every one of us; we are never separated from the

Wisdom and Power that flows through us, as it does through all Nature.

• The world is the incarnation of a thought.

Applying the Principles

1. Take a moment to look out your window and appreciate whatever you can see of the natural world. If it's just the sky, look at that. If there are trees against the sky or a few plants on the ground, look at them. If you have a beautiful view of water, sky, and greenery, soak it in and consider yourself blessed indeed!

2. As you're looking, contemplate the depth of the sky. Think about how many millions of miles your line of sight is traveling and what wonders lie beyond your current vision. Consider the complexity of the tree or plant you're looking at. Ponder how many millions of cells are working together to make up what you see and how they interact with the air, the soil, and the sunlight to maintain themselves and grow.

3. Close your eyes and *feel* Nature working for your good. Feel the air moving around you, refreshing itself for your next breath; feel the way your body relaxes into the chair, resting itself for your next burst of energetic movement. Consider that the food you've eaten is being converted into that energy; consider how your next meals are growing, all the ways the food is coming to you, all the people producing all the things that make your life work. It's all Nature's process going on inside and all around you, for your benefit.

4. Make it a point to go several times a week to a place where you can experience Nature's beauty and processes. Allow the

experience to relax and refresh you and to bring your thoughts and feelings into harmony with your true nature.

For Advanced Practice

Consider that everything you can see is some combination of energy and matter, responding to your thought to form everything you can see, feel, touch, and taste. What are your thoughts and feelings bringing into form? What would you like to bring into form instead? How can you achieve that? For further reading and learning you can watch the Double Slit Experiment in What the Bleep!: Down the Rabbit Hole (http://www.whatthebleep.com/trailer/drh-trailer.shtml).

Notes

1. For an elegant and readable description of how all matter and energy is based on the interaction of these two tendencies, try *The Quantum Self: Human Nature and Consciousness Defined by the New Physics*, by Danah Zohar (New York: Morrow, 1990).

2. The usual translation of Buddha's first Noble Truth: "suffering exists," is not the literal translation of the Sanskrit syllables. The Englishmen who translated the Sutras did the best they could with the mental framework they brought to the task. Much in the same way, the familiar "Our Father" is not the literal translation of the Aramaic prayer that Jesus taught his disciples to say, and "new order for the ages" is not the only translation of *novus ordo seclorum.*

II
SPIRITUAL LAWS

*Emerson was concerned that society teaches us to focus on problems.
He knew that if we can learn to pay attention to our inner wisdom
and follow its guidance instead, then we need not experience pain
or distress and can live a life of abundant satisfaction.*

LIFE IN ACCORD WITH OUR TRUE NATURE

No Need to Be Dazed and Confused

Our young people seem to struggle constantly. It's as if their minds
have become diseased. Their education is the reason; they've been kept
occupied with political, philosophical, and theological problems that
are irrelevant to their experience. They spend hours considering con-
servative versus liberal, the nature of evil, "original sin," the benefits of
diversity, and the like. These are the soul's equivalents of the mumps,
measles, and chicken pox—and no one knows how to cure them.

The natural mind doesn't know these illnesses. For those who live
according to their own true nature, who aren't concerned with issues
that aren't really theirs to consider, the mind is kept free of such
impurities. In truth, the experiences we don't call (or include in)
education are often more precious to our development than all
the formal studies and examinations we work so hard to complete. The
regular course of studies in my years of academic and professional

education have provided me with no more useful facts than what I've gained in some idle reading on my own.

No one need ever be perplexed nor ever have difficulty working things out, regardless of their level of education on a subject. A few strong instincts and simple rules are all we need.

Those who live life from within have a rare self-knowledge, a deep strength. They can describe their faith clearly, as well as their experience of union and freedom. They're open to inspiration. If everyone does and says only what comes from within, only what's in harmony with her or his own true nature, then doubt or confusion is impossible.

The Gift of Inspiration

There's far more inspiration and far less intention and planning in history than we admit. Even Napoleon and Caesar found more power in following their nature than in any deep-seated, farsighted plans. Extraordinarily successful people have always refused or minimized praise, saying they didn't warrant it. They've even built altars to whatever deity they held responsible for the success of their actions, because they knew that their success lay in their willingness to set aside the mental chatter and open their minds to the unobstructed flow of inspiration. To the outside viewer, the resulting deeds seemed to be that person's, but the individual was merely the channel.

Clearly, inspiration and insight are invaluable, but they're gifts beyond our control—I've never been able, by my own will, to inspire myself—and formal education does its best to thwart and eliminate our capacity to receive these gifts.

The Ease of a Life Based on Our True Nature

Our society teaches us to sacrifice ourselves for the sake of others. The education system and media are built around the notion that giving up some aspect of our own life is a good thing. As a result, our schools, churches, and charities too often become burdens on a community, causing pain for its members and donors and pleasure for no one. There are natural ways to accomplish these organizations' intentions, but we don't utilize them, so we don't arrive at our goal. For example, we don't all need to give money to charity. Sometimes giving our skill or our produce directly to those in need is easier and more useful than giving our cash to an organization.

In another example, why do we require all children to attend school? It's natural for children to inquire and for adults to teach, but this can be done whenever the questions are asked. There's no need to shut young people against their will in a cramped classroom for hours at a time. Historically, most children spent several hours a day with an adult in their own homes, yards, and businesses, learning to think and do what the adults around them thought and did. Then as teenagers, if they had mastered the three Rs (Reading, wRiting, and aRithmetic) and wanted more education, they would leave the home and go to a college to get more depth in philosophy, the classics, and the sciences. The rise in homeschooling may be partly due to a recognition of the effectiveness of this ancient approach. Children who are allowed to follow their own natural inclinations to learn become lifelong learners, and for those who learn to do the right thing as a natural part of growing up among people who are modeling it, it's spontaneous, rather than something they have to figure out in each situation.

We all love people who seem to embody spontaneous good. The less someone thinks about doing the right thing and just does it, the more we like him or her. When we see someone who naturally acts in ways that are graceful and pleasant, we feel compelled to thank God that people can be like that. They, meanwhile, simply *are*. But we can't become good people by any act of will. Many people talk as if struggling is virtuous, saying that someone who struggles must be better than others, but that's not how it works. God, as a symbol of what is good, is either here or not.

This makes all our rules and laws and expectations and social norms—the shoulds, oughts, musts, have-tos, and got-tos (five of the most toxic words in our language)—seem a travesty. They're like a wall built to keep out invaders who have no problem leaping over it. Society's rules and assumptions about "normal" are as ineffective in our lives as federal bureaucrats trying to address local issues, when the self-governance of town meetings does the job perfectly.

As we consider all this, we must accept that our success is a function not of our education or socialization but of our willingness to rely on our own innate wisdom. And as we continue this line of thinking, we realize that there's really no need for struggle, no need to despair. We're led directly to the realization that our own lives could be far easier and simpler than we make them and the world could be far happier than it is.

We begin to see that we've made our own distress by relying on inadequate reasoning rather than on the wisdom that is our true nature. We've set up processes based on our poor understanding of how the world works—our shoulds—that have trapped us in their own unfolding. By blocking the wisdom that flows through us, we've blocked our own good life, and we see this most clearly when we walk out of a meeting or business transaction into some natural beauty. It's as if Nature herself is reminding us how difficult we've made our lives.

Instead of making life hard, let's be like Nature, which always works by the most direct route. When the fruit is ripe, it falls. When the fruit has been released, the leaf falls. Even the cycle of water is simply falling. Walking, on two legs or four, is falling forward. And the earth, moon, sun, comets, and stars all fall forever and ever.

Our Choices

Why work so hard at choosing your place, your work, your relationships, and your activities? There's a place and work for you that fits perfectly and feels right, but it won't be found by comparison and analysis. Instead, place yourself in the middle of the stream of power and wisdom that energizes all who float in it, and you'll be carried to your perfect contentment.

There's one perfect direction in which all doors open. Like a ship on a river, with obstructions on every side but one, we find that every block is removed on that one side, and we sweep serenely into an endless sea of possibility and delight.

What I'm really suggesting is not to choose based on your perceptions or senses. The hand, the eyes, and the appetites are not the whole of a person. What I call right or good is the choice of my *whole being*—my inner, true nature. What I call heaven, and am constantly seeking, is a state or environment that my whole being longs for. And my own work will always be the activity that satisfies every aspect of my being, for the good of all.

Our Right Work

Each of us is called to do something unique, to make our own individual contribution to the universal pattern, and no one has any other call. We're all inclined to do things that are easy for us and result in good for us and others, but that no one else can do. If no one else can do the work we've been called to do, we have no rivals; there's no competition. By doing our own work, we create a need in the world that only we can fulfill; we create the taste by which the public enjoys what we produce.

Knowing this, it's time to hold people responsible for their choice of work. It's no longer acceptable for someone to excuse his or her actions as "normal" in their line of work. The mess on Wall Street and the Enron scandal are the result of just such excuses. Why would anyone work in a job where they're supposed to be dishonorable? Is that anyone's true calling? And since each of us has a calling, a vocation, we all have hidden potential that is pulling us toward endless joyous activity. Our talents are the call to that vocation. By doing what is truly ours to do, we blossom.

In any situation, we can take every opportunity to communicate whatever we know and think, or whatever we consider worth doing, so the people around us can begin to know who we truly are. Until we are truly blossoming and can communicate ourselves to others in fullness, though, we've not yet found our true calling. And if the work we're doing right now is not ideal, then we're called to be more than the situation. We can, in our thoughts and actions, make it a richer experience for ourselves and everyone else.

Our Potential

How ridiculous to take on the meanness or rigidity of the work one does instead of converting it into a growth experience!

Human beings are a process, a progressive unfolding and expansion of potential. Sadly though, too many people tend to fit themselves as well as they can into the daily details of the work they fall into and keep repeating the same pattern over and over. There's a big difference between someone who has taught the same material over and over for twenty years and someone who has been teaching and learning for twenty years, or even someone who's built a hundred different houses and someone who's built the same kind of house a hundred times. When repeating the same patterns over and over, such people become part of the machine; they are lost.

People tend to fall into ruts because they like others' approval. We accept the way other people do things and don't see that things could be done divinely instead. Or we look for greatness in the organized and familiar, not remembering that the hero always arises out of the pitiful company in which he was hidden and that a master violinist uses catgut to make a Stradivarius sing. What society calls obscure, mean, or wretched is merely a condition or situation whose greatness is not yet exposed, but that you, following your calling, could make as famous and enviable as any could be—just like Mother Teresa did in the slums of India.

No one, therefore, is extraordinary, nor is he or she ordinary. All are uniquely individual. Everyone has his or her own genius, the particular quality that distinguishes each of us from all others. To be a good person is to be contented with our own individual nature. I love and honor the great Greek hero Epaminondas, but I don't wish to be him. It's better to love my own world rather than his, and you can't bother me by saying that he acted while I sit. I see action to be good when needed and sitting still to be good as well. If Epaminondas was the man I take him for, he would have happily sat still if he were living my life instead of leading the Athenian troops against Sparta more than two thousand years ago. I won't turn away from the immensity of good that is my life just because I've heard that it comes to someone else in a different form.

We don't need to be concerned about whether we'll accomplish enough to meet some social expectation of greatness. Our highest ambitions are directly proportional to our skills, so as we follow our own inner guidance, we'll find that we are truly satisfied with our accomplishments.

Our Always Visible Character

In every group we enter, in every action we attempt, we are measured and labeled. Even troops of boys, whooping and running through the yards, accurately weigh and measure a newcomer within a few days. A pretender may sit on a throne forever, but he will be seen for what he is because while pretension may sit still, it cannot act. Pretension has never produced an act of real greatness; it never wrote an *Iliad*, abolished slavery, or created the Internet.

There need never be any doubt about the respective ability of human beings because each of us is seen for what we are worth, and if anyone knows for sure that they can do something well—that they can do it better than anyone else—all others automatically agree. No one need ever be deceived. The truth will be known; even our bodies speak it. So even when we try to hide, we cannot. What we are engraves itself upon our face, our body, and our fortunes in letters of light. Every glance of our eyes, every smile, every hello, every handshake is a confession. If someone is untrustworthy, people may not know why they don't trust him or her, but that won't change the fact that they don't. If someone has a vice, it affects his eye, shapes his cheek, forms lines around his mouth, and sets the number of the beast on the back of his head; it writes, "Oh fool! Oh fool!" on the forehead.

Our own character, therefore, is always announcing itself. If you act, you show your character; if you sleep, if you sit still, you show it. It's impossible to conceal our character; therefore, boasting is useless.

You may think, because you've not spoken and have given no opinion, that others are curious as to what your verdict might be. But no; your silence answers loudly. Your companions have learned that you can't help them. You haven't tapped your inner wisdom; you have nothing to offer to help them understand more clearly what they wish to know.

Don't be an excuse for humanity, bowing your head and justifying yourself with made-up reasons. Why should I dodge and duck and cower with unreasonable apologies, as if my being here were impertinent? What is this false modesty? Why do we pretend to be less than we are? Shall I not take the place that I was born to?

If you visit your friend, why apologize for not having done so earlier, wasting your friend's time and defacing your own act of visiting now? You're making the visit now. Let that friend feel that the highest love has come to visit. Why torment yourself and your friend by secret self-reproaches that you've not helped up to now? Be a gift and a blessing. Shine with real light, rather than borrowing the light of gifts.

All the goodness that there is in our words and actions will be revered. As much virtue as there is in us, all of it will be seen by those around us. A sincere word is never completely lost. A generous act has never fallen useless; some heart always greets and accepts it unexpectedly. Thoughtful, generous people who are devoted to spiritual principles will always instruct and guide humanity.

So the hero has no fear that a brave act will go unnoticed or unappreciated if he doesn't acknowledge it. Someone knows it—he himself—and through that knowledge he experiences a peace and nobleness that is a better proclamation of the fact than telling the world about it.

Our Communication and Works

When anyone speaks the truth in the spirit of Truth, the eye is as clear as the heavens. When someone is trying to hide something or seeks to harm another, the eye is muddy, blinks rapidly, and sometimes squints. That which we don't really believe, we can't really say, though we may repeat the words over and over. The great Swedish seer Emanuel Swedenborg told us that this is so even in the spirit world.[1] He described observing a group in that world trying to articulate something they didn't believe. They could not do so, no matter how they tried to push their mouths and lips into the necessary shape.

I've heard an experienced attorney say that he was never concerned about the effect a lawyer who didn't believe in his or her client might have on a jury because the lawyer's disbelief will be seen by the jury and, despite all protestations otherwise, that disbelief will become the jury's disbelief. Similarly, if a teacher has any opinion he or she wishes to conceal, the pupils will learn it as thoroughly as anything said aloud. People feel your opinions and react to them without being able to say how and why they do so. Just as the mathematician can figure the whole circle from a small arc, we are always reasoning from the seen to the unseen.

So while to speak and be understood seems the simplest of things, it may also be the strongest of ties, since to be understood by another links us to that person. A spiritual and mental bond may be formed that is stronger than we had expected—or appreciate. We teach by being our true selves and doing what is ours to do, but there is no teaching until the student is brought into the same realm of consciousness as the teacher. In that state, something like a transfusion takes place; the teacher's thought and the student's thought become one thought. And no future experience can take away that learning or its benefit.

This is the process that brings the viewer of a work of art into the same state of mind that the artist was in when the art was made. This is how deep wisdom is shared by seekers of remote ages, even when the secret meaning is buried deep within the pages of a book. Not even Plato's secret doctrine could be hidden from a Francis Bacon or an Immanuel Kant. So Aristotle says of Plato's works, "They are published and not published."[2]

This principle applies to all communication. Those who can communicate who they are can teach, but not by words; one must teach by doing. Those who can give teach, and those who can receive learn. The way to speak and write what will not go out of fashion is to speak and write sincerely. Those who write to themselves write to an eternal public.

A work of the intellect is empty if it is mere words. It must affirm itself or no logic or oath can support it. The writer who takes his subject from his ear, rather than his heart, should know that he has lost as much as he seems to have gained. Even though half the people praise its beauty and genius, it still needs fuel to make a fire. Only life can transform life, and we can be valued only as we make ourselves valuable.

When we hear that Dr. So-and-so or Ms. Such-and-such is delivering a lecture and we have learned that they do not communicate their own characters, that their ideas go in one ear and out the other, we don't attend; the lecture would be an escapade, not a communication. If we have reason to think we might experience their deeper expression, we would go through all kinds of inconvenience to attend. Others would bring their sick on stretchers to hear the Master speak, and we would do the same. Moses and Homer stand forever, and though every generation has only a few individuals who actually read and understand Plato, his words are always printed and available to all. True teachers have a real impact, and the communication of their character can withstand critiques and time.

Our Right Action

We can say the same of every action: its effect is measured by the depth of feeling it comes from. The great men of history rarely knew they were great; it took a century or two for that fact to become evident. They did what they did because they couldn't *not* do it; it was the most natural thing in the circumstance of that moment. Such is the genius of our true nature.

The actions of great men are simply demonstrations of what is possible for all of us. They are the particulars, showing us the direction of the stream we all flow in. Today, though, we call people inactive when they don't go to a job every day and bring home a paycheck. We adore institutions, not realizing that they are founded on our own thoughts.

This worship of size and scale permeates our culture, like other irrational beliefs and superstitions of the senses, but the real action of life is in silent moments. Our lives are not determined by the visible choices of a job or marriage or acquisition of a public office, and so on. Instead they take form in a silent thought as we walk along a quiet avenue, in a momentary idea that transforms our lives, an inner voice that says, "You've done that, but it could be even more wonderful if you do this." All the years that follow stem from this single thought, and every aspect of our lives is shaped by it. It's a constant force that affects a lifetime.

Ideally, every moment of our lives would be driven by these moments. Every aspect of our being would be so clear, so unobstructed, that all aspects of our lives—our work, our religion, our diet, and so on—would be an authentic picture of our true nature. Unfortunately, though, most people are not that well integrated; the light of our nature doesn't shine through, and those observing us are often puzzled by the disconnects and discontinuities in our words and actions.

Why should we be impressed by the word action? It's a trick of the senses—no more. Why should we run about as busybodies and superheroes? Action and inaction are alike to the Great Soul. We know that every action is born in a thought, but still, our poor minds don't consider themselves to be anything unless they see some outward appearance affirming their worth. They need some special diet, fashionable coat, soul-stirring prayer meeting, volunteer board, great donation, high office, or some visible action to testify that they're worth something.

If we must have great actions, let's make our own actions great. All action tends to expand, so let's do one thing that is a fine expression of who we are in the place the Soul has put us. For me, that means focusing on my own responsibilities. Why do I need to read a novel or play video games before I have completed the tasks I've agreed to? How dare I read of Washington's military campaigns when I've not answered the letters or emails sent by my own friends and relatives? To allow ourselves to be entertained when we've not dealt with what's in front of us doesn't serve us or our community. And there's always some contribution that is ours to make; we need never be bored, need never be like the young man who, to paraphrase Lord Byron, "didn't know what to do, so *he watched TV.*"

And it's far better that I do my own work than that of others. The tendency to focus on other peoples' work is to underestimate the value of our own, and it comes from ignoring the fact that everyone's fundamental nature is the same. We desert our own work when we focus on our neighbors and their needs; we might as well be Peeping Toms. Surely my time, my relationships, my paperwork are as important as theirs!

The fact that I'm here shows me that the Soul had need of my being here—and I don't want to disgrace the Soul. Why would I imagine that I should be in another place, trying to find fulfillment in another way, assuming that the Soul didn't know its own needs? Heaven is large, with space for all kinds of love and courage. If the Great Soul incarnated as a poor woman and in her sad body went out and swept rooms and scrubbed floors, still its light could not be hidden; sweeping and scouring would instantly appear the peak and radiance of human life—as it did with Mother Teresa and her Missionaries of Charity.

To think is to act. The truly rich man lies in the sun and sleeps; *being* his true nature.

Essential Points

- No one need ever be confused or ever have difficulty working things out, regardless of their level of education.
- Extraordinarily successful people have always been willing to set aside their normal thoughts and open their minds to the flow of inspiration. We've blocked our own good life by blocking the wisdom that flows through us.
- Our success is a function not of our education or socialization, but of our willingness to rely on our own innate wisdom.
- There's one direction in which all doors open for us; our talents and gifts are the call to that vocation.
- Each of us is called to do something unique, and no one has any other call. We're all inclined to do things that are easy for us and that result in good for ourselves and others, but that no one else

can do. Because only we can do it, we have no rivals; there's no competition.

- People feel your opinions and act out their consequences without being able to say how and why they do so. When the student is brought into the same realm of consciousness as the teacher, a mental transfusion takes place; the teacher's thought and the student's thought become one thought.
- The effect of every action is measured by the depth of feeling it comes from; only Life can transform life, and we can be valued only as we make ourselves valuable.
- Ideally, every aspect of our being would be so clear, so unobstructed that whatever we're doing—our work, our religion, our diet, and so on—would be an authentic picture of our true nature.
- To think is to act. The truly rich man lies in the sun and sleeps; *being* his true nature.

Applying the Principles

1. Look at your calendar and to-do list. Underline the tasks that are on them because you think you *should* do them. Put a big star around the tasks that are there because you can hardly wait to do them. Circle what is there because you think it isn't possible to experience what you want to without doing these tasks first.

2. What experiences in your life have given you the deepest satisfaction, the greatest thrill, the loveliest beauty? Make a list of at least seven such events. Next to them, answer these questions: Were they items that you bought or ones that you already own? Were they natural wonders? Were they things or activities you created or gave to others? Now consider how you can have more experiences such as these. Write down two or three possibilities.

3. Make a list of all the activities that come easily, that are *effortless* for you to get started on, that you *enjoy* doing, and that you feel *energized* as you do them (these are based on the 3 *Es* described in a study of successful entrepreneurs at Stanford Business School in *Creativity in Business* by Michael Ray and Rochelle Myers). They can be from any aspect of your life. If you have difficulty thinking of these activities, either walk through or visualize each room in your house, the garage, the yard, your workplace, the marketplace, or any favorite vacation spots. List the activities (including play!) in any of these spaces that you truly enjoy and are energized by. These are your gifts and talents.

4. Create a new calendar and to-do list for the next week made up of activities that you know you enjoy doing and want to do, remembering to schedule time for just being or sleeping in the sun (or shade). How does it feel? What thoughts do you have about this new list compared to the old one? Write down everything that comes to mind, and then cross these words off as you rewrite your list and calendar. Write down what you're thinking now. Do this until your thoughts are either quiet or supportive.

5. For an entire weekend or vacation, do only what, in the moment, feels Effortless, Enjoyable, and Energizing (the 3 *Es*). As much as possible, avoid the shoulds, oughts, musts, have-tos, and got-tos to follow your Soul's calling, to be in the flow. Each time you take a break from an activity, check in and ask yourself: Is this still feeling like the 3 *Es*? Am I in the flow? If your answer to both questions is yes, if you're having a good time and things come together easily, continue. If not, stop and breathe for a minute and find out what feels better now. It may

be time to eat or do something else entirely. At the end of each day, make a list of all that you did and experienced, and at the end of the experiment, compare how much you experienced or accomplished during this time to what you normally would have done: Observe how much better you feel.

For Advanced Practice

Try living from your 3 *E*s calendar for twenty-eight days. If you find doing so means saying no to things you used to do with people, observe whether you feel the need to make up excuses for the change. If you do, remember Emerson's words: "Why this false modesty?" Try saying something like "I've rearranged my priorities, and that just doesn't fit right now," or "I appreciate the times we've had together, but I need to do things differently for a while." Describe your experiences at the end of each week in your journal. Then at the end of twenty-eight days, look at how you feel, how much energy you have, and what you're doing each day. How do they compare with how you felt and did before you began the exercise?

NATURE PROVIDES FOR US

Emerson saw that the natural world is constructed in such a way that if we follow our inner guidance, we can be and have and do all that fulfills us, but that for this to work, we must be who we are called to be by our true nature, our essential selves.

Following Guidance

Being able to observe Nature but not control it, we can see that it's not our thinking that makes things happen in the world around us but a higher process at work. Our every inspiration is the intelligence of the universe offering us the clearest, most direct path to our happiness. There's guidance in each of us. This is because there is at the center of Nature, and in each of us, a Soul. It's so intertwined with universal processes that we prosper when we accept its advice. We need only follow through.

When we obey that inner drive toward our true joy, we become what we've dreamed of. We begin to understand that living from our acceptance of Universal Love relieves us of most of our worries. And as we look even deeper, we see that our struggles are unnecessary and fruitless. We begin to realize that only in easy, simple, and spontaneous action—when we're in the flow—are we strong and effective.

We have in ourselves all the power we'll ever need. What we do we have, so why hope or fear? I don't even have to think much about it to realize that my life truly satisfies me. The good Soul nourishes me and unlocks new enjoyment and power for me every day.

Finding Our Good

Each of us may have whatever is truly ours. From everywhere we may take what belongs to our soul. We can't take anything else—even if all the delights of the world were within our reach. Nor can all the force of the world prevent us from receiving what is truly ours.

Each of us may have whatever support we take, whether we sneak about and deny our own names or whether we see our work as perfect. So take the place and attitude that are truly yours. You may set the tone of your own life; the world must meet it; it will accept your own measure of your doing and being.

Wherever we go we gather whatever is like us for our fulfillment. We choose or reject particular people and circumstances according to what suits us best. Like magnets attracting bits of steel out of a pile of metals, we take only our own out of the infinity of possible experiences around us. These, in turn, determine the qualities of the universe we experience.

Certain facts, words, and people remain in our memories without our being able to explain why. Though these facts, words, and people may not yet be understood, we remember them because they're uniquely related to us. They're symbols of what we believe, showing us parts of our consciousness that we haven't yet explored—and couldn't discover by studying others' writings or works.

Of these, a few anecdotes, a few faces, and a few incidents are much more important in our memories than we would expect by ordinary standards. The memories you treasure are the unique experiences that your own particular gift has brought to you. Let them have their own weight. Don't reject them to replace them with more conventionally acceptable illustrations of your life. Don't hang on to memories or fears that disempower or distress you, either. What your heart thinks is great is your own greatness. Your soul's loving focus is always perfect for you.

Perceiving Our Good

To keep a secret from one who has the soul's right to know it is impossible; it will tell itself. Napoleon sought Austria's secrets, but all the terrors of the French Republic had no effect on the Austrian government until he sent Monsieur de Narbonne, born of an old noble family, with all the morals, manners, and family connections that the Austrian nobility respected. In a matter of days, he had penetrated all the secrets of the Austrian imperial cabinet. His natural right and readiness to know what his peers knew had won out. In the twentieth century, we've seen over and over again, in story and film, how detectives and spies must fit in and seem to be a part of a situation in order to gather the information they seek.

However, none of us can comprehend what we're not prepared to experience, no matter how close we are to it. A chemist may tell all his most precious secrets to a carpenter, but they'd still be safe, though the chemist would never be willing to utter the same information in the presence of another chemist.

We must have a mental framework to make sense of what our perceptions tell us. It's as if Nature protects us from encountering premature ideas; we can't see what's staring us in the face until the mind is prepared. Then we see it so clearly that the time when we could not understand seems like a dream.

Because our perceptions are projections of our mental framework, what we see in the events of the world around us are our own thoughts, feelings, and actions made large. The good and evil we see in the world is in the same proportion as the good and evil we find in ourselves. In this way each of us may read in the world what we write upon it. Likewise, a book is a thousand different books to a thousand different readers. You can take any book that I've read and read your eyes out, but you'll never find in it what I'd found.

To understand this is to realize that the world is actually very empty and relies on the mental framework of the viewer for all its splendors. Soil and water, rock and sky seem to us in one place a glorious landscape; in another, mere dirt. All the beauty that seems to be in the world around us is actually in our minds. We see only what we make of it. Even our business, our habits, our gestures, and the very food and drink we choose simply reflect our own thoughts and feelings, beliefs and memories.

Our dreams, too, are related to our perceptions. Hideous dreams are simply exaggerations of the disturbances of the day. Likewise, what we think of as evil or dangerous people are like shadows lengthened by the late afternoon's sunlight; they are exaggerations of our own form. "My children," said an old man to his boys scared by a shadowy figure in the dark entry, "you'll never see anything worse than yourselves."

So since we can neither see nor have anything more than what we are, let's stop looking outside ourselves to justify our fears or find our good. Let's seek inside ourselves instead, for what is already in our being must emerge and shine in our world as long as we exist.

Our Relationships

Not surprisingly, we're always finding ourselves in our friends and associates. We see the qualities of our own minds magnified in one acquaintance and our emotions in another. We cling to one person and avoid another according to how like or unlike ourselves we see them to be.

Introduce a thoughtless oaf into a group of gentlemen and he cannot change the group. It's perfectly obvious to all who observe that he is not part of it, though he stands in the same room. The group is uncompromised by his presence. He can't fight the eternal laws of mind that adjust the relationships between all people in accordance with what they have and how they are in the world. Similarly, it's an impossible situation for the simple woman who is enamored of a man's aristocratic appearance but who has none of those admired characteristics in her own thoughts and actions; the two will have no common ground on which to relate. The scholar may forget himself and pretend to be a man of the world to attract the attention of an immature girl, but if he would be his own true greatness, the love of a woman whose serenity and beautiful soul can feed his own will find him. No one is more deeply punished than those who've chosen their relationships based on other people's ideas and expectations.

We may, when we forget ourselves, believe we must associate with people of a certain position or type. But we can only truly be friends with those whose experience seems to mirror our own, whose life seems to parallel ours in some wonderfully refreshing way. A well-known person of great accomplishment or beauty may come our way, and although we may give him or her well-deserved respect, we will still hold that person at a distance. Then, quietly, a person of like mind, a brother or sister of the soul, comes near and we are immediately refreshed by a depth of intimacy that is like new blood in our veins. We always find our own.

The Flow

To be virtuous, to manifest good in our lives, is to act in accordance with the nature of things, and the nature of things is such that the good, the virtuous, always prevails. Goodness or virtue is the ultimate authenticity. It's a perpetual substitution of being for seeming. Remember, Moses' God is named "I AM."

So the lesson in all these observations is to *Be*. Don't seem. Let's make our choices in accord with Nature. Let's unlearn the wisdom of the world and rest in the flow of Nature's power. Let's learn that the power of Truth alone makes anyone rich and great.

Essential Points

- Our every inspiration is the intelligence of the universe offering us the clearest, most direct path to our happiness. There's guidance in each of us.
- We have in ourselves all the power we'll ever need, and each of us may have whatever is truly ours.
- We gather whatever is like us wherever we go, like magnets attracting bits of steel out of a pile of metals.
- We can't see what is right in front of us until the mind is prepared because we must have a mental framework to perceive it.
- Every aspect of our lives reflects our own thoughts and feelings, beliefs and memories; we may read in the world what we write upon it.
- We can see or have only what we are, so let's stop looking outside ourselves for our good and seek inside ourselves instead, for what is already in our being must emerge and shine in our world as long as we exist.
- To be virtuous, to manifest good in our lives, is to act in accordance with the nature of things, and the nature of things is such that the good, the virtuous, always prevails.

- Be. Don't seem. Choose in accord with your own true essence. Why pretend to be less than you are?
- Rest in the flow of Nature's power; the power of Truth alone makes anyone rich and great.

Applying the Principles

1. Remember a time when you felt inspired to say or do something. What did it feel like? How and where did it happen? Did you follow your inspiration, or did you let some inner voice censor it, convincing you it wasn't really OK to do or say anything? If you followed it, what happened? (A great example of this is the part in *The Secret* where Jack Canfield describes how he first followed W. Clement Stone's advice and set a goal of earning $100,000 in a year and what kept him inspired to do it. Note that he got his first inspiration in the shower—which is where most people report hearing the "still, small voice," probably because it's the one place we're not listening to or talking with someone else.)

2. Imagine your life as if everything were perfect: you get up when it feels good, eat what is most satisfying at the time and place you most prefer, do the things that are your gifts, see the people you most enjoy seeing, and so forth. Imagine living a day in that life, a week, a month, a year. Write a description of that life. Does it seem possible? Impossible? Why? Is it a life of true wealth or foolish riches? Can you see how that life might fulfill your soul's purpose? How or how not? If not, how could it do so?

3. For one week, say to yourself every morning as you're getting up, "Today the power of Truth is working for me, so everything that helps me fulfill my life's purpose now comes to me with no effort on my part and with great joy for all concerned." Notice throughout the day the information, resources,

and people that "coincidentally" appear. Each night, just before you go to sleep, make a list of these events and say thank you to the soul of Life (also known as God, the Mother, the Holy Spirit, Allah, and so on) for bringing more good into your life.

For Advanced Practice

1. Set a personal intention that is outside your normal range of activity and is believable to you but beyond anything you know how to do right now. Write it down, with a date of when it will be achieved and circle the date on your calendar. The intention may be about your health, your finances, your relationships, your work, or where and how you live—whatever aspect of your life you're ready to upgrade.

2. Create some way to remind yourself about your intention every day. Make it the first thing you do as you wake up.

3. Spend the first few minutes of every day, as you're getting up, imagining that this intention is fulfilled. *Feel* it in your body and your emotions. See, hear, taste, smell, and touch whatever you can in your imagination that is associated with achieving your intention.

4. Write down, as they come up, any ideas that come to mind that might bring this intention closer to fulfillment. Then follow through on them, even if you can only take it one small step at a time.

5. When you reach the date you'd circled, take a look at how close you actually are to accomplishing the intention you'd

set. You will probably be very close indeed. If so, congratulations! You've let your true self work for you! If not, go back over your written inspirations and ideas. Which ones did you not do? Why? When did you stop believing that you could experience what you had intended?

6. Now, knowing that Nature is working for your fulfillment, do this exercise again with a new intention.

Notes

1. In the early 1700s, Emanuel Swedenborg began to experience trance-visions. His books describing his "excursions" into heaven, hell, and other domains include *Heaven and Hell as Seen and Heard* and *The Heavenly City*. His writings greatly influenced Emerson, as well as Goethe, Wordsworth, and others around the world. To learn more about Swedenborg's life, read *An Introduction to Swedenborg's Religious Thought*, by John Howard Spalding (New York: Swedenborg Publishing Assn., 1966).

2. This line is a clue to Emerson's intentions to bury the "secret" in his diversions and embellishments so only the determined might find it. Interestingly, the early twenty-first century has been prophesied to be when such secrets become widely available.

III

THE LAW OF COMPENSATION

*Emerson could see that the common belief that we're judged
only after death for the things we've done in life can't be true.
He saw that the belief that we don't get back what we
give out keeps people from fulfilling their potential.*

The Fallacy of the Traditional Religious Approach

Recently at church, a preacher respected for his traditional beliefs was
describing the Last Judgment in the usual way. He assumed that wicked
people are successful and good people are miserable, and that judgment
is not executed in this world. He then urged, based on reason and the
Bible, that both groups would be compensated in the next life. No one
in the congregation seemed offended; the listeners went their separate
ways afterwards with no remarks on the sermon.

But what did the preacher mean by saying that good people are
miserable in the present life? Was he telling us that only unprincipled
people have houses and land, offices, wine cellars, cars, fine clothing,
stocks and bonds, cash, caviar, and other luxuries, while good people
are poor and despised? Was he saying that the saints in the hereafter
will be given these things? This must be what he meant, for what else
could he be saying?

Was he saying that good people will have time to pray and praise
in the next life? To love and serve humanity in the hereafter? But

they have the time to do all that now. This preacher made the common mistake of assuming that bad people are successful in this world and that judgment is not executed in this lifetime. He accepted the marketplace's definition of success as having all kinds of toys and luxuries, and he missed the chance to help us learn what true success is. Sadly, he's not alone; most religious writings are similar in this belief.

But most people are better than this theology. Their daily life proves it false. All creative and aspiring souls leave it behind through their own experiences. And people are wiser than they know. If they heard in conversation what they heard from the pulpit, they would probably question it, if only in silence—the thundering silence of an audience's dissatisfaction.

Duality

To understand how we're compensated, we need to understand duality. We find polarity, or duality, in every part of the natural world: in darkness and light, heat and cold, the ebb and flow of tides, in action and reaction, male and female, the inflow and outflow of breath in plants and animals, and so forth. Something resembling man and woman, the ebb and flow of the sea, and day and night is present in a pine needle, a kernel of corn, and in each individual of every species of animal. Make the end of a needle magnetic and the other end becomes its opposite; if the south attracts, the north repels. Each thing is half of what it might be, always suggesting another half to make it whole.

What is true at the largest level is also true at the smallest: the entire system of things is represented in every particle, so the quality of duality applies to the whole as well as every part of the whole. Systems theory tells us that while the whole is greater than the sum of its parts, understanding a part leads to an understanding of the whole. Fractals demonstrate this concept beautifully: a very simple set of lines repeated hundreds and thousands of times yields a very similar design on a grand scale. For example, the complexity of a fern leaf is based on the pattern | /.

Other qualities are maintained across the whole as well. For example, there's a consistent balance of gifts and defects across all species. If one part of a body is oversized, then other parts are reduced, as in an elephant or rhinoceros. Another example can be found in mechanical forces: when we increase power by pressing our foot down on the accelerator, we lose running time or fuel efficiency. We can also see this balance in the compensating movements of the planets; Newton's law of action and reaction is at work across the solar system.

The nature and conditions of individual people can be understood in the same way. Every excess causes a defect, every defect an excess. Every sweet nature has its sour, every apparent evil its goodness. We can say that every faculty that provides pleasure has an equal penalty put on its abuse, making moderation the answer for life.

So in the world of things, for everything you've missed, you've gained something else, and in everything you've gained, you've lost something.

Leveling Processes

Nature, always seeking balance, hates monopolies and exceptions. In the same way that the waves of the sea return to level from their highest crest, natural and social conditions tend to equalize themselves. There's always some leveling process that brings the stronger, overbearing personality down—and the gentler, meeker person up—to the same level as the rest of humanity. It's the Law of Compensation at work.

For example, though one may look at the president as holding a position of power and having fine things, it usually costs him all his peace and the best of his manhood to achieve the White House. In order to maintain for a short time his grand appearance in the world, the man who would be president must bow and scrape before the real masters who stand behind the throne—the party bosses and financial backers and special interest groups who believe they can pull the strings of government.

Genius isn't immune either. Those who, by their will or thought, have earned high positions and now oversee thousands of people are held responsible for all of them. Or if they've been given the light of inspiration, they must always give up the satisfying comfort of sharing it with others if they are to remain faithful to the new revelations of a constantly expanding Soul. The past, tradition, parents—they all become a source of dissatisfaction to those whose gift is the light.

Fame, too, has its leveling compensation. Has anyone acquired all that the world admires and wishes for? Then they must leave behind the admiration of that world. Simply by being faithful to their own truth and their own experience, they watch their names become bywords and their pictures fill the tabloids.

The Law of Compensation writes the laws of cities and nations as well. It's useless to build or plot or conspire against it. As the ancient Romans said, "*Res nolunt diu male administrari*" (Things refuse to be mismanaged for long). Though there may appear to be no checks or balances to a new wrong, they do exist and will appear. If the government is cruel, the governor's life isn't safe. If taxes are set too high, revenues will yield nothing. If the criminal code is too tough, juries will not convict. If the law is too mild, individuals will take their own vengeance.

At the other extreme, if the government is a powerful democracy, there is greater life and energy in the citizens and life glows with a brighter flame. If the individual is benefiting others as much as he or she is being benefited, then both lives are enhanced exponentially.

Wealth is a process, a flow. Those who have riches and use them to increase the flow of abundance in the world have their riches increased in many ways. But if anyone gathers and holds on to too much, the laws of Nature will take out of his or her body what has been stored in the bank.

Omnipresence

Not just duality and balance but all the essential qualities of the universe are present in all its parts. All the senses, movement, resistance, appetite, and organs of reproduction are present in the tiniest creature. The microscope cannot show us an animal that is less than perfect, no matter how small it is.

Every developmental shift is the same process repeated in myriad forms. A horse is understood as a running man, a fish as a swimming man, a bird as a flying man, a tree as a rooted man. Each new form repeats not only the essence of its own type but part for part, all the details, difficulties, energies, and purposes of every other.

In our human experience, every occupation, trade, art, and transaction is related to and contains every other one. We can find in every line of work every aspect of human life—its good, its ill, its trials, its processes, and its purpose. And each one somehow incorporates the whole person and describes his or her destiny.

All these examples, in all aspects of the universe, demonstrate that everything in the natural world contains all the powers of Nature. Everything is made up of one unseen substance. Every quality of the universe is present in every part. The true doctrine of omnipresence is that God, as the soul of Life, exists with all His qualities in every moss and cobweb.

The Law Working

The soul of Life lives and works through all things as the only reality, the balanced and complete whole present in each part. This is why it's said that all things are then added to it: power, pleasure, knowledge, beauty, and so forth. This is the wisdom of Solomon and

of Jesus. From all perspectives, everything is perfectly interconnected—if you see smoke, there must be a fire; if you see a hand, an
arm, or a leg, you know a body is there.

So cause and effect, means and ends, seeds and fruit cannot be
separated. The effect blooms in the cause; it's the fruit in the seed.
Every act rewards itself. The reaction is in the action itself and in the
circumstances surrounding the action. The reaction in the circumstance is often spread out over a long time and may not be seen for
many years, when it is, at last, understood. Then, generally, people
refer to the reaction they see as either great good fortune or retribution, instead of as the reaction that was within the action at the start.

This is because people try to act as if we were separate from the
whole, as if there were parts of our minds and bodies that don't affect
the whole and aren't affected by the whole. We try to be a "somebody," to set ourselves up as separate from the Soul, to have things for
the sake of having them, to be seen for the sake of being seen. If the
Soul says, "Eat," the body chooses to feast. If the Soul says, "Man
and woman shall be one flesh and one soul," the body tries to join
the flesh only. If the Soul says, "Have dominion over all things for the
good of all," the body aims to have power over all things just to satisfy
its cravings.

When we seek pleasure for the body alone, we separate our sen-
sory delights from our other needs; we separate the physical from the
spiritual. Humanity's ingenuity has always been dedicated to having
the one without the other, yet we can no more divide things this way
than we can get an inside without an outside, a light without a
shadow. As systems theory contends, because the universe is one
interconnected whole, you can never do just one thing.

The failure of our attempts to separate these is so obvious that it
seems mad to even try, but it's a disease—an addiction that begins in
our earliest act of rebellion against our parents' rules and infects all
future thought processes. The diseased mind can no longer see the

totality of the Soul in each object. It only sees the potential for sensual delight and not the dissatisfaction built into it. The mind sees the mermaid head but not the fish tail.

Humanity has acknowledged all this in fables, proverbs, classic literature, and laws throughout history: Give and it shall be given to you. He that waters shall be watered himself. Nothing ventured, nothing gained. Who does not work does not eat. If you put a chain around the neck of a slave, the other end fastens itself around your own. Bad counsel confounds the advisor. Basically, TANSTAAFL: There ain't no such thing as a free lunch!

It is so written because it is so in life. In this world nothing can be given; all things are traded.

Working with the Law

The Soul, which within us is a feeling, is Law in the world we see outside us. We feel its inspiration within; we can see its movement and power out there in the evolution of life.

Those who are successful in business pay cash on the barrelhead as they go along because they know that no one who has received a hundred favors and rendered none has really benefited. Has anyone gained by borrowing, through laziness or cunning, their neighbor's products or tools or money? The successful have learned that people often pay very dearly for small frugalities, and borrowers drown in their own debt. Each time someone has borrowed, they've set up a condition of superiority and inferiority, and every further transaction is based on the earlier one. They may find that the highest price we can pay for a thing is to ask for it.

The wise know that it's best to pay every reasonable demand on your time, your talents, or your heart as it comes due. Always pay, because sooner or later you will pay the entire debt. People and events may stand for a time between you and justice, but justice is merely postponed.

The wise also dread the kind of prosperity that only burdens you with more property to manage; they avoid holding on to too much. Nature's goal is our benefit, but the benefit must be passed on—deed for deed and dollar for dollar—to somebody else. And the benefits we share can't be merely returning to those who've given to us; they must, as with all Nature, expand beyond their origins. Those who confer the most benefits to the largest number are the greatest.

Paying for labor and tools works by the same law. The prudent say the cheapest labor is often the most expensive. When we buy a broom, a mat, or a knife, we use good sense to fill a need. Likewise, it's best to pay well for a skillful gardener, tailor, mechanic, or business manager with good sense and a good reputation.

Our labor, in all its forms—from sharpening a stake to building a city or writing an epic—is the clearest demonstration of the Law of Compensation. The absolute balance of give and take—the fact that everything has its own price and if that price is not paid we receive something other than what we had sought—is no less sublime on a spreadsheet than in all the action and reaction of the natural world.

The real payment for our labor is knowledge and good character, of which wealth and good credit are mere indicators. Money can be lost or stolen but knowledge or character cannot. I've no doubt that the high laws and consistent principles that each of us sees in whatever processes we work with improve our work and, though we rarely say it, actually make it feel more important and effective. So follow the law of Nature: Do the thing and you shall have the power; those who don't do it won't have it.

And as in all the rest of life, there can be no cheating; swindlers swindle themselves. The beautiful laws and substances of the world work to persecute and punish whoever would seek to confound them. These individuals find that things are arranged to support truth and benefit all who abide by Nature's laws, but there's no den in the world to hide a rogue. Commit a crime against Nature, and all the world is glass; the very substances of the natural world—snow, wind, water, gravity—become penalties to those who would take without giving. You can't take back the spoken word; you can't draw up the ladder or wipe out the traces—some condemning event always happens.

On the other hand, all right action is equally rewarded. Love and you shall be loved. All love is mathematically balanced, just like an equation.

Full Protection Under the Law

Thoughtful people find that Absolute Good (which, like fire, turns everything to its own nature) surrounds them like a shield so that no harm can even touch them. Instead, just as armies sent against the always-victorious Napoleon threw down their weapons and became his friends, so apparent disasters of all kinds, from illness to storms, carry blessings to the good and loving person.

The same Law that guards us from harm can defend us from selfishness and fraud as well. We don't need to protect ourselves from others; prisons are not the best of our institutions, and shrewdness in trade is not a mark of wisdom. People suffer their whole lives under the false belief that they can be cheated, but it's as impossible for anyone to be cheated by anyone else as it is for a thing to be and not be at the same time. We must accept St. Bernard's wisdom that "Nothing can work me damage except myself."

There is a third silent party to all our bargains. Nature, in the Soul of things, guarantees the fulfillment of every contract. Honest service cannot lead to loss, so if you work for an ungrateful employer, work all the harder. Put God in your debt and every effort shall be repaid. And the longer it takes to be paid, the better it is for you; compounded interest on top of compounded interest is this bank's rate of return.

The Benefits of Challenges

Even thoughtful, caring people are befriended by weaknesses and defects. No one has ever had a point of pride that wasn't also a source of injury; likewise, no one has ever had a defect that wasn't somehow made useful. We're all like the stag in the fable who was proud of his antlers and hated his feet; when the hunter came, the stag was saved by his feet, only to be destroyed by those antlers when they tangled in a thicket.

Every one of us needs to thank our faults. Our strengths grow out of our weaknesses. If a man has such a temper that he's unfit for society, he learns to entertain himself, learns to be self-reliant, and thus, like the wounded oyster, mends his shell with a pearl.

None of us has a thorough understanding of the talents and trials of others until we've seen the triumph of our own talents and suffered through our own trials. That's why a great man is always willing to be little. Sitting on the cushion of his advantages, he's bored. When he's challenged, he has a chance to learn something; he gets to use his wits and his strength, he discovers his ignorance and conceits, he develops skill, he becomes compassionate.

In general, every evil we don't succumb to is a benefit. Just as some ancient warriors believed they took on the strength and courage of the enemy or beast that they killed, so we gain the strength of whatever apparent evil we overcome. That's why wise people engage directly with their assailants. It's an opportunity for them to find their own weak points. And while whatever minor wounds have been inflicted in the process will fall away as dead skin, these people can emerge stronger than before.

Beyond Circumstance

Realizing that everything has a dual aspect, every action its compensation, I've learned to be content. But the doctrine of compensation is not a doctrine of indifference. It doesn't work to sit back and think,

"What difference does it make what I do? If I gain any good, I must pay for it; if I lose any good, I get another." It is, instead, a doctrine that, as we consider it, lifts us above the tyranny of circumstance.

All the evidence tells us that circumstances don't matter. Our true satisfactions seem to have nothing to do with the greatest hardships or delights in our conditions; they're present in all kinds of situations. Under all conditions, even for people living on garbage heaps and in the streets of India, joy can be experienced. For the poorest of the poor, to have enough for the day is a source of joy and satisfaction; nothing else matters. Under all governments, the influence of an individual's character remains the same—in South Africa and New York alike. Even under the despots of ancient Egypt, people appear to have been as free as their culture could make them.

Under all this sea of circumstances flows a deep current of Being. Being is the essence of all that is—the Vast Affirmative, self-balanced, swallowing up all parts, relations, space, and time within itself. Nature, Truth, and Goodness flow from this essence, this primal being.

All that we call darkness, vice, evil, or falsehood is simply the belief that goodness is absent. They're the background illusion the living universe paints itself against, having no power, no capacity to act, for they don't exist in any form at all. They are, in Carl Jung's term, the shadow. They're the illusions of danger projected onto the green screen in video productions, around actors who are, in fact, perfectly safe and comfortable in the studio.

Sometimes as we look at the world around us, the criminal often seems to get away with the crime. There's no stunning confrontation, no crisis or judgment anywhere in the visible world. But to the extent that anyone carries a wrong, an anger, a lie within their own minds and bodies, they are cut off from the flow of life that is Nature. At some point, in some way, they will be required to understand what they have done to themselves and others, but even if we never see that experience, the reduced flow of Life in them is consequence enough.

At the same time, and by the same mechanism, we see that it's not possible for any increase in goodness to be paid for by any loss. There is no penalty for doing the right thing or for experiencing wisdom; their increase is part of the natural flow of being. When I act in accord with Nature's law, I'm in the flow; I add to the world; I Am; I roll back the illusions of darkness and chaos. There can be no excess to love, knowledge, or beauty when they are considered in their purest sense. The Soul refuses to set limits.

The Soul's life is a progression, not a static state. We speak of someone who demonstrates the presence of Soul as "more" than another. The brave man is greater than the coward; the true, kind, or wise teacher or merchant is more of a person than the fool or villain of whatever station. There is no tax, no requirement to return to Nature the good that results from being in the flow of goodness, for that is the income of absolute existence, which we call God.

All material good has its cost, and if it comes to me without my earning or paying for it, it's not truly mine and will be blown away in the next wind. But all the good of Nature is the Soul's, and so it is mine already, and may be had by simply opening my head and heart in alignment with it. So I no longer wish for material goods that I haven't earned; I no longer long for that pot of gold, with all its burdens. I no longer wish for specific possessions, honors, powers, nor relationships; the gain in them is only an appearance, while the cost is certain. But there is no cost for the knowledge that compensation exists and that digging up treasure may not be as desirable as it seems, so I rejoice with an eternal peace, safe from engaging in that particular mischief.

Hidden Blessings in Apparent Loss

All apparent inequalities of circumstances and condition are resolved in the qualities of the Soul. As we look at the world, it seems that the greatest tragedy is the distinction of more and less. How can Ms. Less not feel the pain, not feel indignation or hatred toward Ms. More? We look at those who have less and feel sad, not really knowing what to do. We avoid looking them in the eye; we half expect them to scold God. Their lot seems like a great injustice.

But take a closer look and these huge inequalities vanish. Love reduces them like the sun melts ice. When the heart and soul of all humanity are understood as being one, this bitterness of "theirs" and "mine" is ended. If I feel overshadowed and outdone by great neighbors, I can still love; I can still receive. And those who love make whatever they love their own. Beware, though; to love does not mean to covet. Love is an eternal condition of appreciation, openness, acceptance, respect, and willingness to let be. Only those people and things we feel this way toward are our own.

This is how I learn that my brother is my guardian, acting for me with the friendliest of intentions, and that the home that I've admired and envied is actually mine. The Soul appropriates all things. Jesus and Shakespeare are fragments of the Soul, and by my love I conquer and incorporate them into my own consciousness. Jesus's virtue—is that not mine also? Shakespeare's wit—if I can't make it mine, it's not wit!

We can say similar things about calamity. The transforming events that come along periodically to break up our prosperity are announcements of Nature's Law of Growth. Every individual soul must, by this law, leave behind all the things, ideas, rules, and assumptions that held it firmly in place so it can move on. We must be like the shellfish that crawls out of its beautiful stony home because it no longer fits and then slowly forms a new house.

If someone is full of life and vigor, these transforming events are frequent, until, in some wonderful state of consciousness, these undoings of attachments become unceasing. Then all worldly relations hang very loosely about that person, like gauze, rather than the impervious garment most people are imprisoned in. Then there is constant development, until it's hard for the self we are today to recognize yesterday's self.

This releasing and undoing would ideally be our constant state—removing dead circumstances day by day and renewing everything in and around us always—yet most of us choose resting, not advancing, and resisting, not cooperating with the divine expansion. We idolize the old and familiar, so growth comes as a shock. We can't part with our friends; we can't let our angels go. We don't see that they only go out so that archangels may come in.

People don't believe that anything that might happen today or tomorrow could compare with or re-create that beautiful yesterday. They don't believe in the Soul as eternal and omnipresent. Like the Israelites arguing with Moses in the wilderness, they linger in the ruins of the old tent where they used to have food and shelter, not believing that Spirit can feed, cover, and energize them again. They can't stay among the ruins but won't rely on the new, so they walk forever looking back to the past. But clinging and weeping are useless. The voice of the Almighty shouts, "Up and onward forevermore!"

So, long after a calamity, we reach an understanding. Even though whatever loss we experienced—of health or child or love or property—seemed to be un-repayable at that moment, years or months later, it seems to be the genius act of a wise guide. It transformed our way of life, ending one stage of growth that was ready to be done, and allowed the formation of new relationships, properties, or work more suitable to the next stage. What was once an inconsolable loss is now a blessing. Like a butterfly that has struggled to emerge from its cocoon or a bird that must break open its shell, we are now free to fly and touch thousands of lives; like a plant moved out to the garden from the greenhouse, we now have room for our roots and sunshine for our heads—enough to provide shade and fruit for the whole community of humanity around us.

Essential Points

- Those who have riches and who use them to increase the flow of abundance in the world have their riches increased in many ways.
- Cause and effect cannot be separated. The effect already blooms in the cause; it's the fruit in the seed. Every act rewards itself. You can't do wrong without suffering wrong or do good without receiving good. Every opinion reacts back upon the person stating it.
- Everything has its own price, and if that price is not paid, we receive something other than what we had sought. Always pay whatever is due, for sooner or later you will pay the entire debt.
- Nature's goal is our fulfillment, but the benefits we receive must be passed on to someone else. The greatest people are those who provide the greatest benefit to the most.
- We don't need to protect ourselves. Good people find good surrounding them so that no harm can even touch them. The same law that guards us from distress in every disaster defends us from selfishness and fraud.
- All that we call darkness, vice, or falsehood is the background illusion the living universe paints itself against. These illusions have no power.
- The true doctrine of omnipresence is that God, as the soul of Life, exists with all His qualities in everything everywhere, always.
- A deep current of being flows under all circumstances as all life, all wisdom, all beauty, and all good.
- When I act in accord with Nature's law, I'm in the flow; I add to the world; I roll back the illusions of darkness and chaos.
- All material good includes its own dissatisfaction and has its cost. If it comes to me without my earning or paying for it, it's not truly mine. But all the good Nature offers is already mine and totally fulfilling.

- Calamities are actual announcements of Nature's Law of Growth, whereby we leave behind all the things, ideas, rules, and assumptions that held us firmly in place and move on. Their intensity depends on how hard we cling to the past. And in time, even what was once an inconsolable loss is now a blessing.

Applying the Principles

1. Pick up a magnet and play with it. Notice that while there's no separation between the two ends, they attract and repel in opposite ways. Consider a coin. Notice that the head and tail can't be separated; they're intrinsic parts of the whole. How is your life like these objects?

2. Do something special for someone or remember a time when you did something as a gift for someone else. How did you feel as you were planning it? How did you feel as you were preparing it? What did you learn from planning and preparing it? What was the recipient's reaction? How did it make you feel? What benefit did you take away from the gift you gave to another?

3. Emerson wrote that Absolute Good protects good—that we don't have to be afraid of what others, or Nature, might do to us—and many others have said that what seemed to be the worst thing that could happen turned out to be a blessing. As you look back on times when you experienced events that felt hurtful or damaging, what benefits came to you in the process? What kind of growth did you experience? What new opportunities opened up?

4. Consider the ways the really rich live: Warren Buffett, one of America's wealthiest men, has not moved from his old house or

changed his simple habits for decades. He sees his wealth as something to be used, not hoarded or thrown away on trinkets and temporary delights. Oprah Winfrey, one of the world's richest women, has a beautiful home near the city where she works and one where she vacations, and she spends much of her time and money on projects she believes will make a difference. Both of them continue to do what they've always done in a way that generates income for themselves and supports the people who work with them and for them. This is the case with Bill Gates, Prince Charles, and the Kennedys as well. How do you share the benefits you receive? Do you invest in others' well-being? If you knew that sharing more meant receiving more, what would you be doing with what you're receiving now?

For Advanced Practice

If you could structure your work or your business to maximize the benefits to others while living the 3 Es (Effortless, Enjoyable, Energizing. See chapter 2) for yourself, what would your life look like? Is that a direction you can imagine moving in? Do one thing in that direction each day for a week and write down what you did (and any results you experienced) in your journal.

IV

HUMANITY AND THE OVER-SOUL

*Emerson saw that people who allow a higher wisdom to guide them
accomplish far more with far less effort. He understood that, instead
of being separate individuals with individual souls, we are fully
interconnected outlets of one Over-Soul that functions outside space
and time and that ensures that we receive all the knowledge
and resources we need for our fulfillment.*

Our Source

As I consider my life, I must acknowledge a higher origin for its
events than the will I call mine. The same goes for my thoughts. I can
desire, I can look up and become receptive, but the visions and
answers come from some place outside my normal, waking self. So
I've come to think of humanity as a stream whose source is hidden.
When I watch that river of life and inspiration flowing into me from
someplace I can't begin to see, I understand that I'm a receiver of my
life, not the cause.

Just as the earth lies within the soft arms of the atmosphere,
humanity is also surrounded and embraced. We are part of a unity, an
Over-Soul, in which each individual being is contained and made
one with all others.[1,2] This Over-Soul is our common heart. We
experience life in parts—as particles and particulars—but within each
of us is the soul of the whole, the wise silence, the universal beauty,
in which each part and particle is joyfully connected: the eternal
One. And this deep power in which we exist, whose blessings are

totally available to us, is self-sufficient, whole, and perfect in all ways and for all time.

So the seer and the seen, the subject and the object, both being part of the whole, are one. The Soul is seeing itself through us and as us. We may see the world piece by piece as the sun, the moon, the animal, the tree, but the whole—of which these are shining parts—is the Soul.

Beyond Space and Time

The Soul measures in one way and the senses and reasoning measure in another. The Soul surrounds everything; being outside of time and space, it contradicts all experience. Time, space, and even Nature are dissolved in the Soul's wise knowing. Time and space are simply reflections of the force of the Soul, even though we've been deluded by our senses into believing that they are real and insurmountable. So Spirit can crowd eternity into an hour or stretch an hour into eternity.

We can get a sense of this by considering our personal experience of time. We all know that there's another measure of age that is separate from our calendar age. We find thoughts of universal and eternal beauty that keep us young. Give us a strain of music or a profound idea, and we are refreshed. Or give us a book of ancient wisdom and we experience a lengthening of our own life. The teachings of Moses, Buddha, Lao Tzu, or Jesus are no less effective now than when they were first spoken, because deep, inspired thought makes itself present through all ages.

The Soul has no dates, no rites, no specialties, no people; the Soul knows only the Soul. The things we consider fixed shall detach themselves from our experience and fall one by one like ripe fruit. The landscape, the buildings, Boston, London, institutions, and society—indeed the whole world—shall in time be blown away like puffs of smoke. All the while the Soul looks steadily forward, creating a new world before her and leaving old worlds behind her. The web of events is the flowing robe she wears.

Growth and Development

The Soul doesn't develop in steps or a smooth line but shifts suddenly from one state to another, in quantum leaps. Like the caterpillar becoming a butterfly, the totality becomes something it has never been before.

So when someone steps up to a new level of genius, it's not simply that he or she is brighter than one person, and then another, and then others, but it is that this person has expanded beyond whole populations in a single surge of development. With each divine impulse, the mind breaks through previous limitations and comes out into eternity, breathing in inspiration and breathing out new possibilities for everyone. There, the mind meets with all great minds, speaks truths that have always existed, and feels more familiar with ancient philosophers than with the people who share their household.

This is the law and process of our character's development as well. What appears to be a simple improvement in character moves us into a place that contains not just one particular quality or virtue but all the qualities of the Divine. For some, it's not even necessary to try to improve. Speak to the heart, and the man becomes virtuous; give a thoughtful child room to act and see all the virtues naturally expressed. As a result, we almost feel as if we compromise a little to speak of the need to be better people or to develop just one of these virtues.

The intellect follows the same law. Those who are capable of humility, justice, love, or hope can immediately grasp the sciences and arts, speech and poetry, action and grace. These two can't be separated. To master virtue is to attain mastery of mind and vice versa. The heart that abandons itself to the One-Mind has access to both general and particular forms of knowledge and power.

The Soul in Humanity

One way the Soul may develop is by taking a form, by incarnating into a body. We live in a society with people who answer to the same thoughts we think or who are obedient to the same great intuitions we live by. We can be certain of their common nature; we see its presence in them. And these other souls, these apparently separated selves, stir new emotions in us—the ones we call passions: love, hatred, fear, admiration, pity, and so forth. From these emotions come conversation, competition, persuasion, cities, and war. We can learn from these results or be destroyed by them.

When we were young, individual people and things were all we could relate to, but with experience, we have come to see the common nature that is in all humanity. Through our experience with individuals, we have begun to experience the qualities that are present in all. We may refer to it as a third party, a common nature that is present in the individuals. That third party, however, is impersonal, beyond persons; it is what is called God.

So we're not really the normal description of humanity; we're not simply biological beings who eat, drink, count, and plant; that's a misrepresentation that we find hard to respect. Instead, a human being is the façade of a temple where all Good and Wisdom dwell.

The Soul is not an organ of the body, but It is what animates and energizes all the organs. It is not a function like memory or the ability to calculate, but Soul uses these mental functions to accomplish Its own ends. It's not the intellect or the will but the master of the intellect and the will. It's not a quality of the person but a light within, a light that shines through us, upon the world around us, and leads us to realize that we are nothing and the light is all. It's the background of our being—an immensity that cannot be possessed.

When the Soul breathes through the intellect, we call it genius. When It breathes through the will, we call it virtue. When It flows through affection, we call it divine love. In the brief moments that the Soul's faith comes to us, we call it Power. (That Power is why we can always ignore the argument that people too often make against someone's extraordinary hopes or dreams—namely, the argument of lack of experience. No past lack can limit our future possibilities!)

Just as there's no line on a magnet where one pole begins and the other ends, there's no wall in the Soul where man—the effect—ceases and Soul—the cause—begins. We lie open to the essence of our spiritual nature, with all the attributes of God. No human being has ever risen above these qualities—Justice, Love, Freedom, Power. They tower over us, especially in the moment when our self-interests tempt us to deny them.

Wisdom and Truth

Most of the wisdom of the world is not wisdom. In fact, the wisest people are not writers or philosophers and would not be interested in fame or celebrity. Most scholars show no spirit; they have a knack or skill rather than inspiration. They have a light, and although they've no idea where it comes from, they call it their own. Their talent is too often some overgrown or exaggerated mental faculty, which makes their strength a disease. Among people like this, intellectual gifts seem more a vice than a virtue, and we feel that their talents get in the way of their experience of Truth.

But the Soul perceives and knows only Truth. As I read a book or hear someone speak, the useless thought is cut away by that very Soul, while the true thought awakens a sense of the whole Soul in me, as Truth always will. Only Wisdom itself can inspire people, and when it does, behold! All present will feel the power of Truth in the words.

Blindness of the intellect begins when we forget to let the Soul shine through, thinking that the intellect itself is sufficient. Weakness of will begins when people try to be something apart from the Soul.

All reform aims, in some way or another, to let the Soul have Its way through us.

If we really pay attention to the words and images of our lives, we can begin to catch many hints of the Soul's secret. As we observe our conversations, our daydreams, our times of passion and remorse, hints of Truth show themselves. In our dreams we often observe ourselves in disguises that magnify and enhance our internal state so we can see it clearly. And as we collect these bits and pieces of light, they begin to broaden into knowledge and brighten our search.

Then we discover that we're wiser than we believe we are. We realize that if we would stop interfering with our true thoughts and act authentically, at the level of Soul, we would always know the thing we seek. If we would simply allow the Soul to speak, we would know whatever we've been searching for along with everything else—and all of humanity, too.

This is why where people engage in heartfelt listening and speaking, the participants become aware that their thoughts have risen to a new level; they all feel deeply connected with what was said. This is true dialogue. All the participants become aware of rising to a higher level of being; therefore, they all become wiser than they were.

The Maker of all that is stands behind us and casts omniscience through us, over the world we see. As a result, the Soul's vision, which we call Wisdom, can read the future and interpret the past. But only by yielding to the spirit of prophecy that is innate in all of us can we know what that Wisdom is saying. (So everyone who speaks from that consciousness sounds crazy to those who don't!)

Recognition and Distinction

Who can explain how they know the character of their friends? No one can, yet none of us are surprised by our friends' actions and choices. In one person, though we've heard nothing bad, we put no trust. In another, though we've met only a few times, we're sure that we can place our trust without concern. We know each other very well. We know whether what someone says he or she is doing is just a hope or if it will come to fruition; who thinks only of himself or herself; and who has the well-being of the whole in mind.

It's an unconscious ability we all use. All our social and economic activity is one constant flow of such evaluations. Thoughts come into our minds and leave them through avenues we never voluntarily opened. Because of this ability, and despite our efforts or imperfections, the unique gift that is in each of us is evident to all. That which we are we shall teach—not intentionally but involuntarily. Our character teaches more than the mind can fathom.

Everyone, in small ways and often against their will, displays all the qualities of his or her character and spirit. And wisdom lies in not judging others but rather in letting them judge themselves while we simply observe what they've decided and respond accordingly.

Everyone's spiritual and moral development is also obvious to all. The tone of someone who is seeking something is not the same as that of someone who has it. Not age, breeding, companions, books, actions, nor talents, nor all of them together, can prevent us from being deferential to a spirit higher than our own. If someone has not yet found his or her place in the universe, everything about this person—manners, forms of speech, turns of phrase, and even opinions—will confess it. If, on the other hand, this person has found his or her center, the light of the Soul will shine through him or her, and all disguises of ignorance, temperament, or circumstances can't hide it. Many books, TV shows, and movies have illustrated this difference. From *The Keys to the Kingdom* (with Gregory Peck), *Zorba the Greek* and *The Shoes of the Fisherman* (with Anthony Quinn) to *Star Trek: The Next Generation* (with Patrick Stewart) and *Tuesdays with Morrie* (book by Mitch Albom; film with Jack Lemmon), the difference in those who have found their center and those who haven't is clear.

Genius

The Soul's omniscience flows into the intellect and makes what we call genius. True genius is spiritual. It is a larger share of the common heart and soul of humanity, not something strange or unusual. In all great writers and poets there is a wisdom that's far greater than any talent they use. That Wisdom shines in Homer, in Chaucer, in Shakespeare, and in Milton. They are content with Truth. They may seem cold and slow to readers who are used to the frantic passion and violent tones of inferior but popular writers, but they have allowed the informing Soul to flow through them, seeing through their eyes and blessing the things It has made.

The difference between men of the world who are considered accomplished speakers or writers and the occasional fervent mystic is that one group speaks from without, as spectators acquainted with the topic, while the other speaks from within, as having had the experience or been integrated with the topic. Jesus and the Buddha speak always from within and in a way that transcends all others—that is the miracle. We all seek such a teacher. So it's of no use to preach to me from without; I can do that too readily myself. If someone doesn't speak from within the veil, where the word is one with the speaker and the topic, then let him or her confess it and let us move on.

The great writers and speakers let us feel our own wealth, so we can pay less attention to their compositions. Shakespeare carries us to such a lofty level of intellect that he points us to a wealth far beyond his own. Then we feel that the splendid works he created, which usually seem to be the peak of possibility, are no more real or useful than the shadow cast by a traveler on the roadside.

At those moments we realize that the inspiration expressed in *Hamlet* and *King Lear* could be expressed just as wonderfully by anyone at any time. The word *inspiration* comes from the word *spirit*, which in the original Greek and Latin referred to breath. So *respiration* is breathing again, *expiration* breathing out, and *inspiration* breathing in.

Why, then, should I act as if those works were the source of wisdom, as if we didn't all have access to the same Soul from which they emerged?

We Receive Our Own

The things that are really yours are pulled toward you. Truly, every word that's spoken anywhere in the world that you need to hear, you will hear at precisely the moment you are ready for it. Every saying, every book, every idea that will help or comfort you will surely find you. Every friend who is craved, not by your fantasies but by the great and tender heart in you, will embrace you.

You may run around looking for your friends, but remember to let your feet run, not your mind. If you don't find your friends, can you accept that it's better that you not find them at this moment? For in truth, there's a power in you that would bring you together now if it were for the best.

This happens because the heart in you is the Heart in all. There is not a valve, not a wall, not an intersection anywhere in nature. One blood flows, uninterrupted, in endless circulation through all human beings, as the water of the Earth is all one sea, and in truth, all tides are one ebb and flow.

The Highest dwells within each of us; the source of the world around us is in our own mind.

Revelation

The Soul doesn't just share information with us; It shares Its very Self, or rather, It passes into us and becomes the person It is enlightening, or It may take us into Itself. We call this experience *revelation*, and such moments always fill us with a sense of the sublime. As with any form of teaching, this is really a merging of minds—the Divine mind into our mind—an ebbing of our individual rivulet into the flowing surges of the sea of life.

Every direct experience of the central source of being fills us with awe and delight. A thrill passes through everyone receiving a new truth or observing a great event that comes out of the heart of Nature. At these moments, the power to see is no longer separated from the will to do; the insight proceeds from acceptance, and the acceptance proceeds from a joyful perception.

We always remember every moment that we experience. We may call it the anointing, a revival, a visitation, or a vision. It may range from ecstasy, a trance, or a prophetic inspiration to the faintest glow of delight—the glow that warms all of humanity and makes society possible.

Then let humanity experience the revelation of all nature and all thought. These revelations are answers to the Soul's questions, not the questions the intellect asks. The Soul never answers in words but in the very thing that is being asked about. An answer in words is always deluding; it's no answer at all to the question you're really asking.

Revelation is not a telling of fortunes or a forecast of the future. In the past, oracles were asked questions about material life—how long someone will live, what they'll do, who else will be involved in their life. But we must avoid this kind of curiosity. The Soul, which is eternal, has no tomorrow and concerns Itself only with cause and effect. The veil that prevents us from seeing tomorrow is not a decree of God but a part of our own true nature that teaches us to live in this eternal moment now.

So don't seek descriptions of the countries you're sailing toward. The description can't change your experience, and tomorrow you'll arrive and know the answers anyway. The only way to discover what the future holds is to float with the tide of being that flows into the secret of Nature, working and living in accord with it. As we do so, without our awareness, the Soul integrates the cause that we now are into a new series of effects, and the question and answer become one.

The Soul is wiser than the things It's made of, and It only descends into the individual It can fully possess. It comes to the lowly and simple; It comes to whoever will put off what is foreign and proud; It comes as insight, as serenity and grace. And when we see those who've been lifted by Soul, we experience new heights of greatness.

People come back from that revelation and possession changed. They no longer care about others' opinions; instead, they search us for our own authenticity. They require us to be plain and true. They have no rose-colored glasses, nor do they seek admiration. They dwell in the present moment, fully experiencing everyday life, simply because of the power of this moment, and the fact that they have become porous to divine thought and to drinking in this wonderful sea of light.

The only way to have that experience is to cast off your disguises and deal with the naked truth in plain confession and omniscient affirmation. Only when we have broken our god of tradition and abandoned our god of rhetoric or good deeds may God, as the soul of Life, fire the heart with Its presence.

To know what the great Soul says, each of us must, to paraphrase Jesus, "go into his closet and shut the door." Each of us must listen solely to ourselves, withdrawing from all forms of other people's devotion. Even the prayers of other people won't work for our good until we've made our own connection.

The simplest person who wholly focuses on and praises the divine becomes divine—yet, forever and ever, the inflow of this better and universal Self is new. How wonderful to experience the fullness of being in that lonely place within, wiping out the scars of our past mistakes and disappointments! It doubles the heart—no, the heart is made infinitely larger, growing to a new infinity in every direction. It inspires an infallible trust: these people no longer just believe but see clearly all that is good and true. They easily dismiss all uncertainties and fears and know that in time, all concerns are resolved. They are sure that their well-being is the Soul's desire for them. They're so overflowing with a reliance on the law of Life that their new sense of being sweeps away all normal goals and ambitions in its flood. They realize that they can't escape from the Good.

Essential Points

- We are part of a unity, an Over-Soul, in which each individual being is contained and made one with all others, embraced and enfolded in Wisdom, Power, Love—all good.
- When we were young, we could relate only to individual people and things, but with experience we begin to see the identical nature that is in all humanity; what is called God.
- The Soul is outside space and time, so even though we've been deluded by our senses into believing that time and space are real and insurmountable, they're simply reflections of the force of the Soul working in us.
- The individual soul doesn't develop in steps or a smooth line but shifts suddenly from one state to another. With each divine impulse, the mind breaks through the shell of previous limitations and discovers new possibilities for everyone.
- Those who are capable of humility, justice, love, or hope are in a position to immediately grasp the sciences and arts, speech and poetry, action and grace. These two can't be separated. To master virtue is to attain mastery of mind and vice versa.
- The Soul's vision, which we call Wisdom, can read the future or interpret the past. By yielding to the spirit of prophecy innate in all of us, we can know what that Wisdom is saying. If we would not interfere with our thoughts but act authentically, we would always know the thing we seek and everything else.
- The Highest dwells within each of us. The source of the world around us is in our own mind; we effortlessly receive all that is ours.
- The Soul doesn't just share information with us but passes into us and becomes the person It is enlightening in an experience called

revelation. It inspires an infallible trust: people no longer just believe but see clearly all that is good and true. They realize that they can't escape from the Good.

Applying the Principles

1. Consider your best ideas. Where did they come from? Where do your everyday thoughts come from? Where does the energy that is the difference between living and nonliving things come from?

2. Remember a time when you and one or more other people were really sharing what was in your hearts and minds and really listening to each other without thinking about anything else (like what you wanted to say in reply). What happened? How did it feel? Take the next opportunity to be with someone in that same way and notice how different it is from your normal conversations.[3] Can you make this kind of dialogue a habit?

3. Take a few minutes each day for a week to contemplate the Over-Soul and its relation to humanity. Emerson considers it a source that wisdom, power, love, and beauty stream from and flow into each of us. Imagine being in one of those streams. *Feel* the wisdom flowing into your mind, the power flowing into your body, the love flowing into—and out from—your heart. Then notice any changes in your thoughts or your body or your relationships and write them down. At the end of the week, review the changes—you'll probably want to do this for a lot longer than a week!

4. One way to know that we're allowing the Soul to work in us and for us is by the number of people, resources, pieces of

information, and parking places that "magically" appear at the right moment. Since the Soul is outside space and time, it's working beyond our reach to get us exactly what our mind is focusing on and bring it into our experience. Make a list each evening of these gifts of the Soul (what Carl Jung called *synchronicities*) and appreciate them.

For Advanced Practice

Set aside fifteen to twenty minutes every morning and evening, six days a week for twenty-eight days, to be alone. For some, this may seem impossible, but if you consider your morning and bedtime routines, your commute, your chores, and your time waiting for others, you'll find there are several times a day when you don't have to be focused on other people. Use some of that time to do some of the exercises in this book (and in other guides for living abundantly), and use one of those times each day to simply be open to inspiration. If possible, look at something beautiful or listen to music for relaxation, or at the least simply feel the warm water of the shower flowing over you. Wherever you are, feel yourself bathed in the radiant fountain of wisdom and inspiration. Let your thoughts wander where they may, returning your focus to the beauty, music, or water as the thoughts drift by. You may want to have pen and paper nearby to catch the ideas that flow.

Notes

1. Charles Fillmore was inspired to call his new movement Unity partly because of this Emerson essay.
2. Emerson's use of the term *Over-Soul* is different from Jane Roberts's (Seth's). He used it almost as Carl Jung uses the term *Collective Superconscious*, saying that all humanity has one common soul that guides and inspires each person, and he generally

used it interchangeably with God. Jane Roberts, on the other hand, described a hierarchy of Over-Souls, with one Over-Soul common to only a few individuals, then another common to a group of "younger" Over-Souls, and so on.

3. David Bohm encourages this kind of exchange in his book *On Dialogue* (London: Routlege, 2004), which is a useful guide for this process. It was first introduced by Martin Buber in *Between Man and Man* (London: Routlege, 2002). Another useful set of guidelines is in Christina Baldwin's *Calling the Circle: The First and Future Culture* (New York: Bantam Books, 1998).

V

The Need for Self-Reliance

*Emerson lived at the beginning of the urban industrial era and saw
many patterns emerging in our culture that even today prevent
people from achieving their full potential. He also saw some
relatively simple solutions to this challenge.*

Society's Limitations

The Power of Individuality

What lovely prophets Nature has given us! We see Her message in the
faces of children and babies, and even some animals. They don't have
the adult's divided and rebel mind, that distrust of the inner sense just
because it doesn't compute with our mind's plans. Their mind being
whole, they still see clearly, and when we look into their faces, we're
often startled. Infancy conforms to no one; all conform to it, which is
why one baby commonly makes four or five infants out of the adults
who play with him or her!

Each stage of development has its own charm, making it enviable
and gracious, not to be ignored. For example, don't think that a youth
has no power if he doesn't speak to us adults; just listen to him with
his friends and he's bold enough! But he knows just how to make
adults unnecessary to his world. This casual acceptance of life is
human nature at its healthiest. A properly cared-for boy embodies

independence, irresponsibility, and the willingness to try and sentence all whom he sees on their merits; he is good, bad, eloquent, interesting, silly, and troublesome. He's not concerned about consequences; he gives an independent, genuine verdict. You must court him; he'll never court you.

A man, on the other hand, is jailed by his concerns. As soon as he has once acted or spoken, he is committed, watched with sympathy or hatred by hundreds whose feelings he must now consider. There is no sleeping pill, no memory eraser for this. Oh, if only he could return to his previous neutrality!

On Conformity

People have become timid and apologetic, no longer upright. They no longer say, "I think," or "I am," but must quote some authority. In this, they're shamed by all other aspects of the natural world, as well as the healthy youth, who are all unapologetic about who they are.

Conformity makes people not just false in a few particulars or a few lying statements but false across the board. Their every truth is not quite true; their two is not the real two; their four not quite four. Their every word is embarrassing, and we have no idea where to start with them.

Most people have no idea what a game of blindman's bluff conformity is. If I know your political party, I know your argument. If I hear a preacher announce that his topic is the usefulness of one of his church's institutions, I know beforehand that he can't say a new and spontaneous word because he has pledged to present only one side of the argument.

Those of us who conform are even dressed in the prison uniforms of the group we've joined. We begin to wear the same clothes, have the same body type, and wear the most absurd expression on our faces—what I call "the foolish face of praise"—the expression we put on when we don't feel at ease, in response to conversations we have no interest in.

To be truly human is to be a nonconformist. But our society is in conspiracy against the powerful individuality of its members. Society is like a corporation in which the shareholders have agreed that in order to ensure incomes for the members, they will surrender their liberty and culture. Conformity is prized above anything else. Self-reliance is not acceptable. Society prefers familiar names and customs over creators and realities; it calls the past sacred.

Nothing, however, is truly sacred but the integrity of your own mind. It's the ultimate measure of things, and if you absolve yourself of any noncompliance with the social norm, you'll find that you have the support of the world. Powerful individuals carry themselves in the presence of all opposition as if everything but their own thoughts and actions were meaningless.

Anyone who would move toward immortality dare not even be limited by anything called goodness but must instead explore whether a thing is, in fact, good. *Good* and *bad* are simply names that are very easily applied to this or that. The only right is what fits your true nature; the only wrong is what is against it.

It makes no difference whether I do what others consider excellent or not. I wish my life to be healthy and sweet, so I avoid the fads and overly rich foods that will lead to diets and treatments. Like many of the wealthiest people in the world (notably Warren Buffet), I much prefer that my life be simple so it can be genuine and consistent, rather than glittering and unstable. I actually am myself, and I don't need anyone's assurance or testimony to feel good. My life is for itself and not a spectacle for others.

All that concerns me is what I'm drawn to do by nature, not what people think. While this rule of thought and action is difficult to live by, it may be what defines greatness. It's made harder by the fact that there always seem to be people who think they know your duty better than you. Keep in mind that it's easy to live by others' opinions when we're out in the world and it's easy to live according to our own when alone, but it's a sign of greatness to comfortably keep the independence of our solitary opinions in the middle of a crowd.

Having said all that, I'm ashamed to say that every decent and well-spoken person who approaches me can persuade me to act otherwise. How easily we give in to names and titles, associations and institutions! I ought to go upright and powerful, speaking the rude truth in all ways. If greed and envy pretend to be philanthropy, should that pass unnoticed? If an angry bigot assumes the cause of human rights and tells me the latest crimes in Africa or China, shouldn't I say to him, "Go home and love your baby and wife, be good-natured and modest to those around you, and never cover up your uncharitable ambitions with this implausible tenderness for people thousands of miles away"? Such comments would be rough and graceless, but truth is more beautiful than any pretense of love. Sometimes I think that our goodness must have an edge to it or it isn't really good.

So don't tell me, as a good man did today, that it's my obligation to find jobs for all poor men. Are they *my* poor men? I think not. There's a group of people to whom, through spiritual connection, I am totally bound. They are my people and I theirs, and I will go to prison for them if needed. But I begrudge every dollar, dime, and cent that I give to people who do not belong to me and to whom I do not belong—including popular charities, the building of community centers, the education of fools, and the thousands of nonprofit associations. Though I confess with shame that I sometimes succumb and give a dollar, it's a wicked dollar that someday I'll be strong enough to withhold.

There are people who perform acts of courage or charity as if they were paying a fine. Their works seem to be an apology or an attempt to pay for their living in the world. It's as if their virtuous acts were penances.

The problem with continuing to do things that are no longer meaningful for you is that it scatters your power. It eats up your time and blurs your individuality. If you support a meaningless church, contribute to a meaningless charity, vote the party line, set your table like a magazine picture, behind all these screens it's hard to detect precisely who you are.

So trust in your true nature and do your own work—that which fits your nature—and the world shall know you. Do your own work and you reinforce your awareness of your Self.

On Consistency

While society's need for conformity is a major block to our development, our own need for consistency is equally damaging. We hold on to our past deeds or words because the people around us have no other way to observe us than through our past, and we're unwilling to disappoint them. It seems to be a rule of wisdom today to bring your past into the present. But why drag around this corpse of your own memory? Suppose you contradict yourself; what then?

This kind of foolish consistency is the hallmark of little minds. It's adored by politicians, philosophers, and preachers, but a great man or woman has nothing to do with consistency. Leave your theory and run. Speak what you think now, and tomorrow speak what you think then—even if it contradicts everything you said today.

"You'll be misunderstood!" say some. Is it so bad to be misunderstood? Pythagoras was misunderstood, and Socrates, Jesus, Martin Luther, Copernicus, Galileo, Newton, and every other pure and wise spirit who ever lived. To be great is to be misunderstood by the conforming public.

And don't be concerned about whether it's possible to violate your true nature. There's a harmony of action and thought in each of us. No matter how different specific actions may seem in the moment, the differences will fade into a harmonious whole over time. Act singly and what you have already done singly will justify you now. Your genuine action explains not only itself but all your other actions.

All willful explorations into alternative ways to express ourselves are brought back into the harmonious process and law of the individual being. For example, if I were to write every day my honest thought without thinking about the future or the past, I don't doubt that it would turn out to be harmonious over a few days or weeks, even though I hadn't meant for it to. Similarly, though the ship's voyage is typically a zigzag of a hundred different angles or tacks, from a distance it appears to be nearly a straight line from port to port.

So let's never again bow and apologize for who we are right now! Let's turn away from the squalid contentment and smooth mediocrity of the times. Let's confront them with the fact that is demonstrated throughout history: that wherever a true human being is, there is Nature at work, the measure of all people and all events; one great responsible Thinker and Actor works wherever a human being works, and a true human belongs in the center of things.

Prayer

In common prayer, people reach outside themselves to some foreign entity, asking for some item, experience, or change in situation to come to them by way of some process that is outside their control. In the process their desire loses itself in an endless maze of natural and supernatural, mediating and miraculous means and ends.

Then there is the kind of prayer offered by a farmer kneeling to weed his garden, the rower kneeling to stroke the oar. The prayers of our actions are heard throughout the natural world, though for small outcomes.

Prayer that seeks a private desire to be fulfilled assumes that the universe is not one being but two. It's based on the assumption that our consciousness is separated from the Soul of the Universe, rather than being all of one piece, so we feel we must do something to bring to us something that is separate from us. As such, it is meanness and theft; it's a vice.

This ends soon as someone experiences the union of the Soul; there is no begging. True prayer is the contemplation of the Truth of life from the highest point of view. It's the heartfelt expression of joy felt by someone who has had a glimpse of the divine Whole, the spirit of God in us pronouncing His works good.

Another kind of false prayer is regret. Discontent is lack of reliance on the Self, a sign of a distracted will. Regret a calamity if doing so helps the person who suffers, but if not, focus on your own union with the Soul, and already the situation will be on its way to repair. Our sympathy doesn't help people, either. Why join them in their tears if your clear statement of Truth would bring them joy and satisfaction?[1]

The secret of good fortune is recognizing the joy in our hands. Those who are self-helping are always appreciated. Doors are opened for them, and they are greeted with honors and embraced with love simply because they don't need help. We celebrate them because they went their own way and scorned our disapproval. As the ancient Persian prophet Zoroaster said, "To the persevering mortal, the Immortals are swift."

Creeds

Every new mind is a new system of thoughts and ideas. If the mind is unusually active or powerful, as with Locke, Lavoisier, Fourier, Freud, Jung, or Einstein, that system is shared with others. The deeper the thought, the more profound its influence on others. Sometimes those thoughts are adopted as a new truth, and new creeds are formed.

But creeds undermine the intellect just as pleading prayers undermine the will. Initially, pupils eagerly subordinate all thought and language to the new concepts, and for a time they feel that the intellect has grown as a result. But in all unbalanced minds, the system is soon idolized and becomes the end rather than a very temporary means. For them, the boundaries of the new thought system blend with the edges of the universe. They think that all the points of light in the universe somehow hang on the arch their teacher built. They can't imagine how anyone who doesn't think as they do can see at all, "It must be somehow that you stole the light from us," they think. They don't realize that light, which has no system and can't be controlled, will break into any mind that is receptive to it.

Well, let them call it their own if they feel it serves them. If they're honest and do well, soon their package of ideas will begin to crack. It will break open, rot, and vanish, and the immortal light in all its glory will beam over the universe just as the biblical story tells us it did on the first morning.

Finding Solutions

As it is now, the power of the individual seems to be destroyed. We've become afraid of truth, afraid of fortune, afraid of death, and afraid of each other.

People drive their cars everywhere, so they have lost the use of their feet. They have watches and clocks but can't begin to tell the time by the sun, moon, and stars. Their books and television shows have impaired their memory, their computers overwhelm their understanding, their insurance companies have increased the number of accidents. And we can question whether some of the machines we use don't actually make life more difficult rather than easier. Even our institutionalized churches can be called into question, since they seem to have encouraged the loss of some vital spiritual energy that was present in the gatherings of early Christians. Where now, in all Christendom, are the Christians? Where, in any religion, are the embodiments of its truths?

We can think of society as a wave. The wave moves onward, but the water it's composed of goes nowhere. People are no greater now than they ever were—and those who were great in the early ages are remarkably like those who've been great in recent generations. Not even our philosophy and science can be said to educate more thoroughly or effectively than that of the ancient Greeks more than 2,300 years ago. The arts and inventions of each period are extensions of current custom; they don't really improve humanity.

Nevertheless, today, people have begun to consider institutions as guardians of the things that really matter. Religious, educational, and governmental institutions are held almost sacred, and to attack any of them is felt to be an attack on the public well-being. People have looked away from themselves and at the things around them for so long that they measure each other's worth by how many things they have, rather than by what each person is.

Our measure of wealth and greatness by the number of things we have has translated into a slavish respect for numbers in general. Political parties—especially in conventions—use the power of large numbers on people's emotions to help their members feel stronger by the presence of thousands of others. Businesses and organizations measure their effectiveness not by how much they've improved society, but by how many customers or members they have.

In each generation, though, a few people have really looked at who and what we are and have begun to become ashamed of many of the things they own—especially if those things have come to them by means they don't feel good about. They begin to feel that such things don't really belong to them, so the things just sit there, unused and unappreciated.

We need men and women who will renovate our lives and our society, but most of the people around us have ambitions way out of line with their abilities and can't even take care of themselves, so they lean, begging, on others. We've not chosen our work, our arts, our religion, or our marriages—society has chosen them for us. We've become party soldiers, fighting with words and shunning the real battles that strengthen us.

If today's young people do poorly, they lose all heart. If our young business owners fail, they are *ruined*. If a fine genius studies at a fine college and is not given a high-paid position at one of the great companies within a year, both the genius and his friends feel he is justified in feeling disheartened and complaining for the rest of his life.

One young person who works through a number of professions—who starts with a garden and "plants it, farms it, peddles it"; edits a paper; sets up and operates a school; runs for city council; and so on, always finding a good way out and moving on to the next calling—is worth a hundred of the others. Such people walk free and proud, not ashamed of not having studied for a profession, because they've lived life, not postponed it. And if any job or position ends, there are a hundred more opportunities, for such as these, not just one.

We need philosophers and teachers who can tell people that they have resources within, that they're not willows bending with the winds. People need to know that they can detach themselves from their circumstances, that by learning to trust the inner Self they'll find new powers. They need to hear that humanity—all of us and each of us—is the Word made flesh, born to shed healing to the nations, and none of us need be the object of another's compassion or pity.

Relying on the inner Self transforms the way people think about things. They have new opinions, new companions, and new kinds of activity. It's easy to see that people who rely on their inner Self must cause a revolution, transforming positions and relations across society.

The moment anyone, relying on the inner Self, acts on his or her own, tossing laws, books, customs, and idols out the window, there will be no more pity. We will thank and revere that one as a teacher who shall restore humanity to splendor, and that name will be held in history's heart. Like Mohandas Gandhi (who led his country to freedom without a battle), Harriet Tubman (who led her people to freedom on the Underground Railroad), Charles Lindbergh (who flew across the Atlantic by himself), Mother Teresa (who cared for those who couldn't be cared for and built a new order in the Roman Catholic Church), and Roger Bannister (who was the first to run a mile in less than four minutes), these individuals will do the impossible so that for those who follow, what was impossible can be normal.

Essential Points

- A child's casual acceptance of life is human nature at its healthiest.
- Whoever would be truly human must be a nonconformist, but society prefers familiar names and customs over creators and realities, calling the past sacred.
- Nothing is truly sacred but the integrity of your own mind. If an idea or activity fits your true nature, it is right for you.
- The problem with continuing to do things that are no longer meaningful for you is that it scatters your power, eats up your time, and blurs your individuality.
- A great man or woman has nothing to do with consistency. Speak what you think now, and tomorrow speak what you think then. Don't be concerned about whether it's possible to violate your true nature. There's a harmony of action and thought in each of us.
- In common prayer, people reach outside themselves to some foreign entity, asking for some change in situation to come to them by way of some process that is outside their control. True prayer

is the heartfelt expression of joy felt by someone who has had a glimpse of the divine Whole.

- The secret of good fortune is recognizing the joy in our hands. Those who are self-helping are always appreciated simply because they don't need assistance.

- People have begun to consider institutions as guardians of the things that really matter. To attack any of them is felt to be an attack on the public well-being. People have looked away from themselves and at things for so long that they measure each other's worth by how many things they have, rather than by what each person is.

- We need men and women who will renovate our lives and society, who can tell people they can detach themselves from their circumstances, trust the inner Self, and find new powers.

Applying the Principles

1. Remember the people in your life whom you've most respected. Did they follow the crowd or rely on their own understanding? Think about the people who've made history and ask yourself the same question. Write down the qualities you've most appreciated in the best people you can think of.

2. Describe two past experiences that didn't go at all well and that you almost wish hadn't happened. How much were you giving your power away to other people, letting their ideas of what was fun or necessary guide you? Write down your answers. Now describe two past experiences that you feel really good about—times when you accomplished something that felt really satisfying. How much did you rely on other people? What new reserves of strength or skill did you discover inside you? Write these answers down.

3. Make a list of the things you do that are no longer meaningful for you. Circle the ones that you do because you believe you should, must, ought to, got to, or have to. Underline the ones that you do because someone else wants you to. Cross out the ones that no longer move you in the direction of your life goals. (These may also have been circled and/or underlined.) What would it take to stop doing them? Make a plan for giving them up over the next twenty-eight days.

4. Make a list of all the people in your life. Next to each name write whatever unfinished business you may have with them. It may be an unpaid debt or favor; it may be a "thank you" or an "I love you"; it may be some old anger or hurt to be amended; it may be returning a book, DVD, or CD. Whatever it (or they) may be, list it. Now consider: Are you willing to do what it takes to be free of this incompletion? If not, why not? Knowing that you're blocking your own wealth and well-being by not finishing these tasks, what small steps are you willing to take to move toward completion? Write these steps down next to each name and consider when you might do them.

For Advanced Practice
Get up in front of a group without any idea of what it is you will be saying. Close your eyes for just a few seconds and feel yourself opening to allow the Soul to express Itself through you. Open your mouth, assured that exactly the right words for this time and place are ready to be expressed through you, and observe what comes out. Notice what feedback you receive from the group after you're done. Write a description of the whole experience in the journal you're using for the exercises from this book.

LIVING FROM THE SOURCE WITHIN

*Having laid out the issues for anyone seeking fulfillment in
our society and the general solution, Emerson provides very
specific guidelines for becoming someone who attracts
wealth and creates well-being.*

The Power of Originality

While everyone in society reminds us of someone or something else,
true individuality, being divine Reality, reminds you of nothing else; it's
the whole of creation. All true individuals are a cause, a country, and an
age in themselves, requiring infinite spaces, resources, and time to fully
accomplish their vision. And as they do so, posterity follows in their
footsteps like a reception line. A man named Julius becomes the first
Caesar, and for ages after we have a Roman Empire. A man called Jesus
embodies the Christ consciousness, and so many minds grow and cling
so closely to his genius that, for millions, he is now identical with all
that is good and possible in humanity. A young physicist named
Einstein equates, and generations of scientists discover a whole new
universe of probabilities.

All our institutions are the lengthened shadow of individuals. All
monasteries derive from one Anthony the Hermit, Protestantism
from Martin Luther, Quakerism from George Fox, Methodism from
John Wesley, and Communism from Karl Marx. All history resolves
itself easily into the biographies of a few strong and earnest people.

Originality and Genius

We always perk up when we come across words and ideas that are
original. The feeling we get from them is more important than whatever the words may say. We call Moses, Plato, and Einstein great
because they set aside books and tradition and spoke what they
thought, not what others said. Like they did, each of us needs to

learn to detect and watch that light that flashes across the mind from within more than we need to study the poets and sages of the past.

Yet most of us dismiss our own thoughts without notice, just because they are ours. Most of us only express a small part of ourselves and are ashamed to consider the divine idea that each of us represents.

Sadly, then, in every work of genius that we encounter, we recognize our own rejected thoughts; they come back to us like a lost treasure. Actually, this is the most useful lesson for us in all great works; they teach us to pay attention to our spontaneous impressions, especially when others are arguing against them. If we don't, then someday a stranger will say exactly what we've felt and thought all the time and we'll be shamed into taking our opinion from someone else.

To believe in your own thought, to believe that what's true in your own private heart may also be true for others, that is genius. Speak your intent with conviction and it becomes the universal sense.

Our Unique Gift

All people are relieved and happy when they've put their hearts into their work and done their best. But there's no peace for those who've done or said otherwise. They've failed to deliver; their muse is silent; their genius deserts them: no invention, no hope.

This is the point in our education when we realize that envy is ignorance and imitation is suicide, and that we must take ourselves for better or worse; it's our lot in life. We begin to realize that the power in our own being is unique, that no one else knows what is ours to do in this life, and that we won't know until we've tried. We understand that this is part of a larger pattern of harmony.

We realize, too, that though the universe is full of good, none of it comes to us if we don't plant it and pick it for ourselves. We come to understand that we're in exactly the right place at the right time for our perfect expression. Our eye was placed where one specific ray of light should fall just so we can testify to the glory of that ray.

Trust yourself! Every heart vibrates to that one note. Accept the place divine Providence has found for you, the society of your peers, the interconnected web of events you're a part of. Great men have always done so, settling childlike into the genius of their age. In doing so, they've demonstrated their own understanding that Trust was seated in their heart, working through their hands, managing their whole being. Sooner or later we must gracefully accept the same transcendent destiny.

True Greatness

A history of great days and momentary victories is what makes a hero great. These days and moments shed a glowing light on the person moving forward with them; a chorus of angels announces them. That's what makes Washington dignified; it's what led Adams's vision to build America. We call it honor. We venerate honor because it's a function of the Self; it's something that has stood the test of time—even when it shows up in a youth.

We've relied on royalty to show us what reverence means. People everywhere have let the king, the pope, the duchess, and the wealthy follow laws of their own. We've let them pay for benefits with prestige instead of money and allowed them to do whatever is clearly good for them. If we consider it thoughtfully, we can see that this has taught us how to acknowledge our own worth and how to express the reverence toward others that is our right as well—and the right of all humanity.

The popular story of the drunk who was picked up off the street, cleaned up, and put in the duke's bed, and on waking was told that he was the duke and had gone insane and must now accept all the honors due his lordship is so well-liked because it symbolizes the true state of humanity. The man on the street who can't imagine he has the capacity to build great buildings or statues feels poor when he looks at such things. To him, palaces and skyscrapers, limousines and libraries are alien and forbidding, seeming to say, "Who do you think you are?" Yet they're all his, seeking his attention, begging him to notice them and own them with his senses. A picture, book, or building waits for my opinion. It doesn't command me; I get to decide whether it deserves praise.

Let us know, then, our true worth. Let's not sneak or skulk, steal or peep, as if we were unwanted orphans trying not to be seen or heard. The world was made for us! We're no longer children, nor invalids hidden in a corner, nor cowards fleeing before a revolution. We are guides, redeemers, and benefactors, continuing the almighty effort, rolling back the edges of the illusory dark and chaos.

Each of us must be so great that we make all our environments nothing. So regardless of apparent circumstances, do what feels right now. The force of character is cumulative; every day you spend doing what fits your authentic nature contributes to the next one. So always ignore appearances. Each time you do so, you make it easier to ignore them in the future.

Self-Expression and Creativity

The Soul created the arts, wherever they flourish. All art is the application of thought to matter within the limits of the situation. The artist saw the model before creating a thing.

Only our Soul can teach us the thing that each of us can do best. No one knows what it is, nor can know, until he or she has tried a variety of things and discovered what comes most readily and uniquely through them. Who could have taught Leonardo to paint or Shakespeare to write as they did? Who could have instructed Benjamin Franklin or George Washington? Who were Francis Bacon's, Isaac Newton's, Albert Einstein's, and Stephen Hawking's masters?

Why do we build our homes according to the norms of another country? If we were to study with hope and love the precise thing that is ours to do, considering the climate, the soil, the length of the day, the wants of the people, and the habit and form of the government, we'd create houses that fit all these requirements and satisfy people's taste and comfort at the same time—just as Frank Lloyd Wright and Buckminster Fuller did and before them the prairie settlers with their houses of sod.

If you can take in what the great writers and teachers say, then surely you can reply to them in the same tone. If you can live your own life fully and follow the guidance of your heart, then you shall bring forth a wonderful, uniquely original expression of divine Creativity.

So insist on yourself; never imitate. You can present your own gift in every moment, and the Creative Force will increase in you in the process. But if you adopt someone else's talent, you will have only a temporary half-possession.

When you do the things that are yours to do, it's not possible to do too much or hope too much. Right now, right here, there's something for you to accomplish that is as grand and brave as the pyramids or Leonardo's paintings or the words of Moses, Rumi, Shakespeare, or Tolkien—and different from all of them, for the Soul would never repeat itself.

Inspiration, Intuition, and Realization

Everyone can tell the difference between intentional thought processes and involuntary realizations, and we all know that we can trust the involuntary realizations completely. Many a CEO has found that analysis can only take us so far, and then we must rely on a deeper knowing, our gut feelings. We may not be able to express them adequately, but we know those feelings are as solidly real as day and night.

Inspiration, quiet and subtle as it may be, is consistent. By contrast, the thoughts and actions I try to control by my own will wander all over the place. Idle reveries, daydreams, the odd emotion—these attract my attention and curiosity.

Thoughtless people don't make the distinction between thoughts and inspired realizations, so they're likely to contradict our realizations, just as they do our opinions. They imagine that we're choosing to realize one thing instead of another, and they're afraid of the realization. Part of them knows that, being an expression of Truth, the realization has the power to change things.

But a realization isn't something we choose. It's not whimsical; it's fateful. If I realize something, my children will realize it after I do, and over time, all humanity will realize it, even though no one may have realized it before I did. They'll do so because my realization, expressed as it is by infinite Wisdom through me, is as much a fact as the sun.

Our Source

Whenever we realize the presence of Truth or Justice, we do nothing ourselves; we simply allow Its rays to pass through us. We rest in the lap of immense Intelligence as it gives us Its Truth and works through us. We call this form of wisdom *intuition*.

What's the source of this genius that we call spontaneous wisdom? It's the radiant fountain of action and thought. It's the source of all inspiration, breathing into us Its wisdom in a way that can only be denied by those who deny all consciousness outside the brain. All things find their common origin in this deep force, this final fact that no analysis can cut through.

We know this when we're resting in our own sense of being, in the Soul. Then we can feel no distinction between things, space, time, or other people. We feel one with them all, and we sense them emerging from the same Source as ourselves. We acknowledge that we share the same life with other beings, and we recognize them as appearances within the natural world, though too often we forget that we share their cause. All things are made sacred in the moment that we are fully present; all things are dissolved into their original formlessness.

This relation between the individual soul and the Over-Soul is so pure that to place any helper, priest, minister, deacon, or chaplain between them is a profanity. If we ask where it comes from, if we seek to understand the Soul that causes all, our philosophers and preachers fail us. All they can do is affirm Its presence.

So if a man claims to know God and speaks of God, we must listen carefully and see if what he says feels true. This seems simple enough, but how many people won't let themselves hear any truth unless it sounds like something in the King James Bible? These people are like children who repeat by rote the sentences of their teachers, painfully remembering the exact words they spoke, never open to learning anything else. So if anyone claims to know and speak with God and uses some old-fashioned language from some other country (which may as well be some other world), don't believe that person. But if he or she speaks clearly and plainly in a way that resonates with both heart and mind, pay attention; the wisdom of inspiration and revelation may well be present.

In the Now

Why do people worship the past? Is the past better than the present? Is the parent better than the child who's been filled with the parent's wisdom and strength on top of her own? Time and space are products of our perception, and history is useless, even injurious, if it's taken as more than a metaphor, a parable of an individual's being and becoming.

The roses under my window don't care about former roses or better roses; they are what they are now. There is no time to them.

They exist, with the Soul, today—simply being a rose. Each one is perfect in every moment. Its whole life acts in the bud, in the full-blown bloom, and in the bare root—no more, no less. Its nature is satisfied, and it satisfies Nature at all moments.

But too often people don't live in the present. They either look back and lament the past, or they ignore the riches that surround them now and strive to foresee the future. They can't be really happy or strong until they live, as all of Nature does, in the present moment, transcending time.[2]

If we live truly, we shall see truly. When we have a new perception, we'll gladly free the memory of all its treasures, letting go of the past as old rubbish. Whenever a mind is open and receives divine Wisdom, all old things—books, teachers, temples—pass away, and the inspired mind lives fully in the now and absorbs the past and the future into the present moment.

Aiming for the Highest

In that moment, that hour of vision, there is no gratitude, nor even joy. Fear and hope are alike in that state, since even hope is less than perfect. When divine Good is near you, when you have infinite Life in yourself, you'll find that the way, the thought, the good that is for you is totally strange and new outside of your previous experience. The individual soul, lifted above sensation and emotion, and outside space and time, beholds Identity and Eternal Causation. It realizes the self-existence of Truth and Right, and rests in the peace of knowing that all is well. Even Power ceases in that moment of rest, since it exists only in the moment of transition from one state to the next, as the Soul develops.

Only to the extent that the Soul is present and unfolding is Its Power active in our lives. As a result, whoever is more reliant on or obedient to the Soul than I, even if she doesn't do or say a thing, must be my teacher, my master. I circle around such people, pulled by a spiritual attraction to their elevated being. This is the principle of the guru in Hindu and Tibetan Buddhist teachings.

In the same way, any individual (or group of people) who allows divine Principle to shape his or her life must then, by the laws of Nature, rule and control his or her whole world. This individual is the master of all the cities, nations, and masses of humanity who have not opened their minds to the divine Principle.

All human activities—commerce, farming, hunting, war, even our speech and body weight—depend on and earn our respect to the extent that they demonstrate the divine qualities of the Soul's presence. And self-existence (simply being I AM) is the fundamental quality of the supreme Cause. So the measure of all lower forms of being, including humanity, must be their degree of self-existence.

So let's become self-existent. Let's bring our attention home and stay focused on the Cause. Let your words, thoughts, and actions tell those who enter your space to take off their shoes, as Moses did and as Muslims do today in a sacred space, because that presence that we call God, the Self-existent, is here within. Let your simple elegance show them the poverty of their glittering worldly fortunes next to the divine riches that all are born with and that we build our world on.

A Solitary Path

It's only as we turn away from the things outside us and stand alone that we can be truly strong and prevail. Anyone who realizes that power is inside us, and that looking outside us weakens us, stands strong and works miracles. Gandhi's work in India is a perfect example; he rarely "recruited" people. He informed thousands through his writings and media appearances and he trained hundreds to use his methods, but he would often start a campaign by simply getting up and doing it, and others would follow because they knew that whatever he did would make a difference.[3]

Activists are weakened by every person recruited to their cause. Is a town stronger than the people who live there? Is a committee more knowledgeable than its members?

So ask nothing of others. As the great Muslim leader, the Caliph Ali said, "Your lot or portion in life is seeking you; so rest from seeking it."[4] Nothing can win your particular race but the eternal principles that have made you who you are and offer you all that is. Nothing can bring you the peace of a truly prosperous life but your own true inner Self.

I like the silent church before the service better than the preaching. How pure and holy everyone looks as they rest in their own private sanctuary! Let's be that way, always.

Sometimes the whole world seems in conspiracy to occupy you with trifles. Friend, client, child, sickness, fear, want, charity—they all knock at once at our closet door, saying, "Come out to be with us!" But stay in your silent space and don't be drawn into their confusion. If others have the power to annoy me, I have given them this power through my own curiosity; no one can come near me unless I let him.

Why should we take on the faults of our friend, spouse, parent, or child simply because they sit at our table or are said to have the same genes as we? All people have my genes, and I have all humanity's. No less than 99 percent of my genes are common to every other member of the species *Homo sapiens*, so that's not a good enough reason to adopt their follies—especially not to the point of shame!

We must go our own way, alone. Our isolation, though, must not be mechanical; it must be spiritual, elevating us to new heights of being. And if we can't rise immediately to our highest state of being— that state of total reliance on and faith in the Self—then let's at least resist the temptation to act contrary to it. We may have to put on the warrior's courage and constancy to do so.[5] We may need such courage sometimes to speak Truth instead of appearing to be hospitable or affectionate.

Give up trying to meet the expectations of the deceived and deceiving people around you. They can't be Self-existent; they do not know Truth. At some point you'll need to write them a letter or simply tell them something like this:

Until now, I've lived with you to maintain appearances, but now I belong to Truth; I obey only eternal Law. I'll make no commitments. I will work to nourish my parents, support my family, to be monogamous in marriage—but I'll do these things in a new way. I release your customs; I must be myself. I can't break myself any longer for you, nor can you for me.

If you can love me for what I am, we'll be all the happier. If you can't, I'll still try to deserve your love. I will not hide my likes and dislikes. I will trust that what is deep within me is holy, and I will do, day and night, only what gives me joy, what my heart calls for.

If you are noble, I will love you; if you are not, I will not hurt you and myself by any hypocritical friendship. If you are true but not living the same truth I feel, then remain with your companions, and I will seek my own.

I don't do this selfishly, but humbly and truly; it's in both our interest, and all people's, to live in our own truth.

This may seem harsh today, but you'll soon love what is dictated by your inner Self as well as mine, and if we follow Truth, it will bring us out safe and together at last.

Will some friends express pain over this? Yes, but we can't sell our freedom, health, or sanity to save their momentary feelings. Besides, everyone has their moments of reason as well, and when they come to know Truth, they'll understand and do the same thing. In fact, many people who've been diagnosed with terminal conditions have found that doing something like this has been an essential step on their path to health and well-being. Fortunately, modern society seems to accept the need for such behavior under such circumstances.

Sadly, though, most people think that the rejection of currently popular social norms is the rejection of all standards of good and propriety, and a few people may use this philosophy to justify their crimes against the Self. But the Law of Compensation remains: we must pay the price or be absolved of it, which may be done directly or through the consequences of our actions. If you decide to pay the price directly, consider whether your relations with your family members, friends, pets, neighbors, and community are complete and whether there's anything that any of them could hold against you. If there is not, you are paid in full and may consider yourself absolved of your social obligations.[6]

For some, it's possible to step outside this circle of obligations by claiming a higher standard, one that simply refuses to label many of society's expectations as obligations. If these people can meet the requirements of that standard, they may dispense with the social expectations. If anyone thinks this is easy, though, let him or her try it for a day. It demands a heroic effort to let go of society's norms and trust the inner Self as a taskmaster. People must keep their hearts high, their will focused and committed, and their vision clear if they wish to let their own inner being function as doctrine, society, and law. A simple purpose must be, for them, as strong as a fundamental necessity is for others.

Off the Wheel of Chance or Fortune

Most people gamble in life, gaining or losing all as the wheel of fortune turns. But you don't have to. You can leave all such games and deal instead with the unchanging law of cause and effect.

So don't believe a word of the news or your neighbors; they judge by always changing appearances. The apparent ups and downs of the events around you have no effect on your life. And as circumstances change and you remain firm in your unique identity, you'll be like a strong column supporting the structure of the community—with no more effort than being your Self.

As you align your intentions with the eternal Will, you acquire what is yours by birthright and stop the wheel of chance. You will have accomplished what the Buddhists and Hindus seek: stepping off the Wheel. In doing so, you are free to be your true Self and to accept your real birthright: the joy-filled and satisfying life of one who knows that you have constant and effortless access to all your needs and desires, for you are the master of a truly abundant world—in fact, of all that is.

Essential Points

- To believe in your own thought, to believe that what's true in your own private heart may also be true for others—that is genius.
- Though the universe is full of good, none of it comes to us if we don't plant it and pick it for ourselves.
- A history of great days and momentary victories is what makes a hero great.
- Insist on yourself; never imitate. If you can live your own life fully and follow the guidance of your heart, then you shall bring forth a wonderful, uniquely original expression of divine Creativity.
- When we're resting in our own sense of being, in the Soul, we can feel no distinction between things, space, time, or other people, and we feel ourselves one with them all. All things are made sacred in the moment that we are fully present; all things are dissolved into their original formlessness.
- People can't be happy or strong until they live, as all of Nature does, in the present, transcending time. The inspired mind lives fully in the now and absorbs the past and the future into the present moment.

- Any individual (or group of people) who allows divine principles to shape his or her life must then, by the laws of Nature, rule and control his or her whole world.
- Someone who realizes that Power is inside us, and that looking outside us weakens us, stands strong and works miracles. So ask nothing of others.
- Give up trying to meet the expectations of the deceived and deceiving people around you. We must go our own way, alone. Our isolation, though, must not be mechanical; it must be spiritual, elevating us to new heights of being.
- That which we are, we acquire. It can't be harmed or stolen, and perpetually renews itself as we breathe.

Applying the Principles

1. Make a list of the most creative people you've ever heard of. Compare it to your lists of the wealthiest and those you most respect. Is there any overlap? Circle the names that are on at least two of your lists.

2. Consider the people in your life today. Are there people in your world you've been leaning on for emotional, financial, or material support? Is anyone leaning on you? If so, is there a mutual benefit; for example, do you count on these coworkers to do some tasks and pay them for it, or do they count on you to help them solve problems and entertain them? Make a list of these names. Have you (or they) become dependent? What would it look like for you to go it alone? What would it take? Write the answers down by each name and note what you're willing to do to lovingly shift away from a relationship of dependency.

3. Write a new description of your ideal life. Describe the qualities of the place you would be living in; the people around

you; the tools, toys, and transportation you'd have or have access to; the kind of community you'd be living in; the quality of the air, water, and landscape around you; the kind of clothing you'd wear, and so on. Now describe your activities— the way you'd be spending your days, evenings, work time, and recreation time. Describe the kind of difference you'd be making in the world around you and how satisfying that would be. Now read over your description and add anything that comes to mind. Now read it again, slowly, *feeling* and seeing each thing. Note how it feels in your body. If anything doesn't feel right, circle it and keep going. After you've finished going through this exercise, redo the circled items until they feel comfortable and energizing. Reread the whole thing, feeling it as you do so.

4. Recognize and appreciate how wealthy you are at this present moment—how much food, clothing, shelter, transportation, and access to information and friends and family you now have—for Nature and our society have given even the modern worker and student much more than most kings of ages past. Make a list of all the ways that you are wealthy now. How did you acquire your wealth? What do you do with your wealth? If you think you'd like to feel wealthier, what can you imagine, using the 3 Es of the previous exercises (Effortless, Energizing, and Enjoyable), would be ways to increase that experience of wealth? What will you do when you feel wealthier? Can you do any of that now?

For Advanced Practice

1. Consider Emerson's letter to his family and friends (on page 96 in this chapter). Essentially he's saying, "I will stay with you and do my best in this relationship, but not because of society's

norms or out of habit. I'm here because I choose to be, and I accept that the Soul has put me here for a purpose that is for the good of all. Don't count on me to stay if that is no longer the case."

2. Now consider your own relationships. Are there people in your life who are there because of social norms or habit? Does staying in a relationship with them feel effortless, enjoyable, and energizing? If not, can you imagine saying no to them a few times? If you can, can you imagine writing a letter like Emerson's to them? What do you think would happen?

3. You can even write such a letter with the intention of not sending it, and get almost the same result. To do so, write a letter to these people in the journal you've been using. As you do so, clearly imagine the person you're writing to sitting in front of you and read the words to him or her as you write them down, sending this person love and appreciation and observing him or her taking the idea in. As you sign the letter, feel the two of you surrounded in the light of love so that nothing is between you except the love. You'll see changes in both your behaviors in direct proportion to how much you've felt the meaning of what you've written.

Notes

1. Emma Curtis Hopkins teaches people just this in her 12 Lessons in *Scientific Christian Mental Practice* (Marina del Rey, CA: DeVorss & Company, 1974), and my interpretation of her work, *Unveiling Your Hidden Power* (Beaverton, OR: Wise Woman Press, 2006). It's the essence of the Science of Mind practitioner's work.

2. What Emerson is trying to help us see here is also the essence of Eckhart Tolle's *The Power of NOW: A Guide to Spiritual Enlightenment* (Novato, CA: New World Library, 2004).

3. Gandhi's method of "nonrecruitment" is lovingly illustrated in the film *Gandhi* with Ben Kingsley—particularly in the second half, when Gandhi leads the Salt March across the country simply by getting up and walking.

4. Alī ibn Abī Ṭālib (Ali, son of Abi Talib) was elected the fourth Caliph (head of the Islamic peoples) a few years after the Prophet Muhammed died. When they were both in Medina, Muhammed told Ali that he had been ordered by God to give his daughter, Fatimah, to him in marriage. In Muslim culture today, Ali is respected for his deep loyalty to Muhammed and his unbending devotion to Islam, as well as his courage, knowledge, belief, honesty, equal treatment of all Muslims, and generosity in forgiving his defeated enemies. Still today, Ali remains central to mystical traditions in Islam such as Sufism and an authority on the Qur'an, the rule of law, and religious thought. This quote is from a collection of verses called *The Sentences of Ali,* translated by William Yule and published in Edinburgh in 1832.

5. The kind of courage and "warrior's armor" that Emerson refers to here is the message in Dan Millman's *The Way of the Peaceful Warrior* (Tiburon, CA: H.J. Kramer, 1984).

6. The Landmark Forum and Werner Erhard's est Training have long encouraged people to "be complete with everyone everyday," so there are no limitations on being true to one's Self.

CONCLUSION TO
INTERPRETATIONS

Ralph Waldo Emerson was the first American to tell us that we are far more than we seem to be, and that we can do and experience far more than we've been led to believe. He came to understand this by studying the work of many others before him, but more important, he integrated the ideas they shared into his own life and thought. He tested these ideas by making choices, taking action, and then observing the effects of these thoughts and actions on himself and those around him. In short, he lived the life that he encouraged us to try.

As we read his words and consider his ideas, we can begin to get a glimpse of how abundantly satisfying a life lived in this way, "from the inside out," might be. We begin to appreciate the beauty of the world we live in without working to make it fit someone else's notion of artistic, neat, or tidy. We begin to see that we can make choices, not on the basis of what our parents, teachers, or any experts have said, but on the basis of what truly feels right for us. We begin to feel the freedom that comes from allowing ourselves to do this. We begin to realize that the whole world exists not as a dangerous or haphazard collection of obstacles for us to overcome, but as a wonderfully supportive environment for us to experiment in. We begin to accept what all the great spiritual teachers of the world have been telling us: Each and every one of us has access to all the wisdom, power, and potential we need to accomplish what is truly satisfying for us simply by paying attention to the still, small voice within and acting on its guidance.

The exercises in this book are designed to help you experience the possibilities that Emerson was encouraging us to see. They're safe ways to experiment with the concepts and to test whether what he said fits into your own life. You'll experience as many results from doing them as you put thought and feeling into them. And if you do them consistently over a twenty-eight-day period, you'll find that your mind is no longer following its old patterns but is beginning to operate from a new set of assumptions, using new thought processes, and so is leading to new kinds of experiences.

Along the way, most people notice many more coincidences, or synchronicities, as their thinking begins to align more with the natural processes of the world around them. People, information, and other resources (including parking places) usually begin to appear at just the right time and place to meet our needs when we do these kinds of exercises. It's as if the universe starts to say, "Well, all right then. Now we're working together!"

The outcome of all this is that we not only begin to know what feels right and fitting for us to do and say and live, but it becomes much easier for us to do and have and be all that we truly desire—which is the definition of a truly abundant life.

Enjoy!

Original Essays

As Emerson and Nature
Originally Expressed

All I have seen teaches me to trust the Creator for all I have not seen.

I

NATURE

There are days which occur in this climate, at almost any season of the year, wherein the world reaches its perfection, when the air, the heavenly bodies, and the earth, make a harmony, as if nature would indulge her offspring; when, in these bleak upper sides of the planet, nothing is to desire that we have heard of the happiest latitudes, and we bask in the shining hours of Florida and Cuba; when everything that has life gives sign of satisfaction, and the cattle that lie on the ground seem to have great and tranquil thoughts. These halcyons may be looked for with a little more assurance in that pure October weather, which we distinguish by the name of the Indian Summer. The day, immeasurably long, sleeps over the broad hills and warm wide fields. To have lived through all its sunny hours, seems longevity enough. The solitary places do not seem quite lonely. At the gates of the forest, the surprised man of the world is forced to leave his city estimates of great and small, wise and foolish. The knapsack of custom falls off his back with the first step he makes into these precincts. Here is sanctity which shames our religions, and reality which discredits our heroes. Here we find nature to be the circumstance which dwarfs every other circumstance, and judges like a god all men that come to her. We have crept out of our close and crowded houses into the night and morning, and we see what majestic beauties daily wrap us in their bosom. How willingly we would escape the barriers which render them comparatively impotent, escape the sophistication and second thought, and suffer nature to intrance us. The tempered light of the woods is like a perpetual morning, and is stimulating and heroic. The anciently reported spells of these places creep on us. The stems of pines, hemlocks, and oaks, almost gleam like iron on the excited eye. The incommunicable trees begin to persuade us to live with them, and quit our life of solemn trifles. Here no history, or church, or state, is interpolated on the divine sky and the immortal year. How easily we might walk onward into the opening landscape, absorbed by new pictures, and by thoughts fast succeeding each other, until by degrees the recollection of home was crowded out of the mind, all memory obliterated by the tyranny of the present, and we were led in triumph by nature.

These enchantments are medicinal, they sober and heal us. These are plain pleasures, kindly and native to us. We come to our own, and make friends with matter, which the ambitious chatter of the schools would persuade us to despise. We never can part with it; the mind loves its old home: as water to our thirst, so is the rock, the ground, to our eyes, and hands, and feet. It is firm water: it is cold flame: what health, what affinity! Ever an old friend, ever like a dear friend and brother, when we chat affectedly with strangers, comes in this honest face, and takes a grave liberty with us, and shames us out of our nonsense. Cities give not the human senses room enough. We go out daily and nightly to feed the eyes on the horizon, and require so much scope, just as we need water for our bath. There are all degrees of natural influence, from these quarantine powers of nature, up to her dearest and gravest ministrations to the imagination and the soul.

There is the bucket of cold water from the spring, the wood-fire to which the chilled traveller rushes for safety,—and there is the sublime moral of autumn and of noon. We nestle in nature, and draw our living as parasites from her roots and grains, and we receive glances from the heavenly bodies, which call us to solitude, and foretell the remotest future. The blue zenith is the point in which romance and reality meet. I think, if we should be rapt away into all that we dream of heaven, and should converse with Gabriel and Uriel, the upper sky would be all that would remain of our furniture.

It seems as if the day was not wholly profane, in which we have given heed to some natural object. The fall of snowflakes in a still air, preserving to each crystal its perfect form; the blowing of sleet over a wide sheet of water, and over plains, the waving rye-field, the mimic waving of acres of houstonia, whose innumerable florets whiten and ripple before the eye; the reflections of trees and flowers in glassy lakes; the musical steaming odorous south wind, which converts all trees to windharps; the crackling and spurting of hemlock in the flames; or of pine logs, which yield glory to the walls and faces in the sittingroom,—these are the music and pictures of the most ancient religion. My house stands in low land, with limited outlook, and on the skirt of the village. But I go with my friend to the shore of our little river, and with one stroke of the paddle, I leave the village politics and personalities, yes, and the world of villages and per-sonalities behind, and pass into a delicate realm of sunset and moonlight, too bright almost for spotted man to enter without novi-tiate and probation. We penetrate bodily this incredible beauty; we dip our hands in this painted element: our eyes are bathed in these lights and forms. A holiday, a villeggiatura, a royal revel, the proudest, most heart-rejoicing festival that valor and beauty, power and taste, ever decked and enjoyed, establishes itself on the instant. These sunset clouds, these delicately emerging stars, with their private and ineffable glances, signify it and proffer it. I am taught the poorness of our invention, the ugliness of towns and palaces. Art and luxury have early learned that they must work as enhancement and sequel to this original beauty. I am over-instructed for my return. Henceforth I shall be hard to please. I cannot go back to toys. I am grown expensive and sophisticated. I can no longer live without elegance: but a countryman shall be my master of revels. He who knows the most, he who knows what sweets and virtues are in the ground, the waters, the plants, the heavens, and how to come at these enchantments, is the rich and royal man. Only as far as the masters of the world have called in nature to their aid, can they reach the height of magnificence. This is the meaning of their hanging-gardens, villas, garden-houses, islands, parks, and preserves, to back their faulty personality with these strong accessories. I do not wonder that the landed interest should be invincible in the state with these dangerous auxiliaries. These bribe and invite; not kings, not palaces, not men, not women, but these tender and poetic stars, eloquent of secret promises. We heard what the rich man said, we knew of his villa, his grove, his wine, and his company, but the provocation and point of the invitation came out of these beguiling stars. In their soft glances, I see what men strove to realize in some Versailles, or Paphos, or Ctesiphon. Indeed, it is the magical lights of the horizon, and the blue sky for the background, which save all our works of art, which were otherwise bawbles. When the rich tax the poor with servility and obsequiousness, they should consider the effect of men reputed to be the possessors of nature, on imaginative minds. Ah! if the rich were rich as the poor fancy riches! A boy hears a military band play on the field at night, and he has kings and queens, and famous chivalry palpably before him. He hears the echoes of a horn in a hill country, in the Notch Mountains, for example, which converts the mountains into an Aeolian harp, and this supernatural *tiralira* restores to him the Dorian mythology, Apollo, Diana, and all divine hunters and huntresses. Can a musical note be so lofty, so haughtily beautiful! To the poor young poet, thus fabulous is his picture of society; he is loyal; he respects the rich; they are rich for the sake of his imagination; how poor his fancy would be, if they were not rich! That they have some high-fenced grove, which they call a park; that they live in larger and better-garnished saloons than he has visited, and go in coaches, keeping only the society of the elegant, to watering-places, and to distant cities, are the groundwork from which he has delineated estates of romance, compared with which their actual possessions are shanties and paddocks. The muse herself betrays her son, and enhances the gifts of wealth and well-born beauty, by a radiation out of the air, and clouds, and forests that skirt the road,—a certain haughty favor, as if from patrician genii to patricians, a kind of aristocracy in nature, a prince of the power of the air.

The moral sensibility which makes Edens and Tempes so easily, may not be always found, but the material landscape is never far off. We can find these enchantments without visiting the Como Lake, or the Madeira Islands. We exaggerate the praises of local scenery. In every landscape, the point of astonishment is the meeting of the sky and the earth, and that is seen from the first hillock as well as from the top of the Alleghanies. The stars at night stoop down over the brownest, homeliest common, with all the spiritual magnificence which they shed on the Campagna, or on the marble deserts of Egypt. The uprolled clouds and the colors of morning and evening, will transfigure maples and alders. The difference between landscape and landscape is small, but there is great difference in the beholders. There is nothing so wonderful in any particular landscape, as the necessity of being beautiful under which every landscape lies. Nature cannot be surprised in undress. Beauty breaks in everywhere.

But it is very easy to outrun the sympathy of readers on this topic, which schoolmen called *natura naturata*, or nature passive. One can hardly speak directly of it without excess. It is as easy to broach in mixed companies what is called "the subject of religion." A susceptible person does not like to indulge his tastes in this kind, without the apology of some trivial necessity: he goes to see a wood-lot, or to look at the crops, or to fetch a plant or a mineral from a remote locality, or he carries a fowling piece, or a fishing-rod. I suppose this shame must have a good reason. A dilettantism in nature is barren and unworthy. The fop of fields is no better than his brother of Broadway. Men are naturally hunters and inquisitive of wood-craft, and I suppose that such a gazetteer as wood-cutters and Indians should furnish facts for, would take place in the most sumptuous drawing rooms of all the "Wreaths" and "Flora's chaplets" of the bookshops; yet ordinarily, whether we are too clumsy for so subtle a topic, or from whatever cause, as soon as men begin to write on nature, they fall into euphuism. Frivolity is a most unfit tribute to Pan, who ought to be represented in the mythology as the most continent of gods. I would not be frivolous before the admirable reserve and prudence of time, yet I cannot renounce the right of returning often to this old topic. The multitude of false churches accredits the true religion. Literature, poetry, science, are the homage of man to this unfathomed secret, concerning which no sane man can affect an indifference or incuriosity. Nature is loved by what is best in us. It is loved as the city of God, although, or rather because there is no citizen. The sunset is unlike anything that is underneath it: it wants men. And the beauty of nature must always seem unreal and mocking, until the landscape has human figures, that are as good as itself. If there were good men, there would never be this rapture in nature. If the king is in the palace, nobody looks at the walls. It is when he is gone, and the house is filled with grooms and gazers, that we turn from the people, to find relief in the majestic men that are suggested by the pictures and the architecture. The critics who complain of the sickly separation of the beauty of nature from the thing to be done, must consider that our hunting of the picturesque is inseparable from our protest against false society. Man is fallen; nature is erect, and serves as a differential thermometer, detecting the presence or absence of the divine sentiment in man. By fault of our dulness and selfishness, we are looking up to nature, but when we are convalescent, nature will look up to us. We see the foaming brook with compunction: if our own life flowed with the right energy, we should shame the brook. The stream of zeal sparkles with real fire, and not with reflex rays of sun and moon. Nature may be as selfishly studied as trade. Astronomy to the selfish becomes astrology; psychology, mesmerism (with intent to show where our spoons are gone); and anatomy and physiology, become phrenology and palmistry.

But taking timely warning, and leaving many things unsaid on this topic, let us not longer omit our homage to the Efficient Nature, *natura naturans*, the quick cause, before which all forms flee as the driven snows, itself secret, its works driven before it in flocks and multitudes, (as the ancient represented nature by Proteus, a shepherd,) and in indescribable variety. It publishes itself in creatures, reaching from particles and spicula, through transformation on transformation to the highest symmetries, arriving at consummate results without a shock or a leap. A little heat, that is, a little motion, is all that differences the bald, dazzling white, and deadly cold poles of the earth from the prolific tropical climates. All changes pass without violence, by reason of the two cardinal conditions of boundless space and boundless time. Geology has initiated us into the secularity of nature, and taught us to disuse our dame-school measures, and exchange our Mosaic and Ptolemaic schemes for her large style. We knew nothing rightly, for want of perspective. Now we learn what patient periods must round themselves before the rock is formed, then before the rock is broken, and the first lichen race has disintegrated the thinnest external plate into soil, and opened the door for the remote Flora, Fauna, Ceres, and Pomona, to come in. How far off yet is the trilobite! how far the quadruped! how inconceivably remote is man! All duly arrive, and then race after race of men. It is a long way from granite to the oyster; farther yet to Plato, and the preaching of the immortality of the soul. Yet all must come, as surely as the first atom has two sides.

Motion or change, and identity or rest, are the first and second secrets of nature: Motion and Rest. The whole code of her laws may be written on the thumbnail, or the signet of a ring. The whirling bubble on the surface of a brook, admits us to the secret of the mechanics of the sky. Every shell on the beach is a key to it. A little water made to rotate in a cup explains the formation of the simpler shells; the addition of matter from year to year, arrives at last at the most complex forms; and yet so poor is nature with all her craft, that, from the beginning to the end of the universe, she has but one stuff,—but one stuff with its two ends, to serve up all her dream-like variety. Compound it how she will, star, sand, fire, water, tree, man, it is still one stuff, and betrays the same properties.

Nature is always consistent, though she feigns to contravene her own laws. She keeps her laws, and seems to transcend them. She arms and equips an animal to find its place and living in the earth, and, at the same time, she arms and equips another animal to destroy it. Space exists to divide creatures; but by clothing the sides of a bird with a few feathers, she gives him a petty omnipresence. The direction is forever onward, but the artist still goes back for materials, and begins again with the first elements on the most advanced stage: otherwise, all goes to ruin. If we look at her work, we seem to catch a glance of a system in transition. Plants are the young of the world, vessels of health and vigor; but they grope ever upward towards consciousness; the trees are imperfect men, and seem to bemoan their imprisonment, rooted in the ground. The animal is the novice and probationer of a more advanced order. The men, though young, having tasted the first drop from the cup of thought, are already dissipated: the maples and ferns are still uncorrupt; yet no doubt, when they come to consciousness, they too will curse and swear.

Flowers so strictly belong to youth, that we adult men soon come to feel, that their beautiful generations concern not us: we have had our day; now let the children have theirs. The flowers jilt us, and we are old bachelors with our ridiculous tenderness.

Things are so strictly related, that according to the skill of the eye, from any one object the parts and properties of any other may be predicted. If we had eyes to see it, a bit of stone from the city wall would certify us of the necessity that man must exist, as readily as the city. That identity makes us all one, and reduces to nothing great intervals on our customary scale. We talk of deviations from natural life, as if artificial life were not also natural. The smoothest curled courtier in the boudoirs of a palace has an animal nature, rude and aboriginal as a white bear, omnipotent to its own ends, and is directly related, there amid essences and billetsdoux, to Himmaleh mountain-chains, and the axis of the globe. If we consider how much we are nature's, we need not be superstitious about towns, as if that terrific or benefic force did not find us there also, and fashion cities. Nature who made the mason, made the house. We may easily hear too much of rural influences. The cool disengaged air of natural objects, makes them enviable to us, chafed and irritable creatures with red faces, and we think we shall be as grand as they, if we camp out and eat roots; but let us be men instead of woodchucks, and the oak and the elm shall gladly serve us, though we sit in chairs of ivory on carpets of silk.

This guiding identity runs through all the surprises and contrasts of the piece, and characterizes every law. Man carries the world in his head, the whole astronomy and chemistry suspended in a thought. Because the history of nature is charactered in his brain, therefore is he the prophet and discoverer of her secrets. Every known fact in natural science was divined by the presentiment of somebody, before it was actually verified. A man does not tie his shoe without recognising laws which bind the farthest regions of nature: moon, plant, gas, crystal, are concrete geometry and numbers. Common sense knows its own, and recognises the fact at first sight in chemical experiment. The common sense of Franklin, Dalton, Davy, and Black, is the same common sense which made the arrangements which now it discovers.

If the identity expresses organized rest, the counter action runs also into organization. The astronomers said, 'Give us matter, and a little motion, and we will construct the universe. It is not enough that we should have matter, we must also have a single impulse, one shove to launch the mass, and generate the harmony of the centrifugal and centripetal forces. Once heave the ball from the hand, and we can show how all this mighty order grew.'—'A very unreasonable postulate,' said the metaphysicians, 'and a plain begging of the question. Could you not prevail to know the genesis of projection, as well as the continuation of it?' Nature, meanwhile, had not waited for the discussion, but, right or wrong, bestowed the impulse, and the balls rolled. It was no great affair, a mere push, but the astronomers were right in making much of it, for there is no end to the consequences of the act. That famous aboriginal push propagates itself through all the balls of the system, and through every atom of every ball, through all the races of creatures, and through the history and performances of every individual. Exaggeration is in the course of things. Nature sends no creature, no man into the world, without adding a small excess of his proper quality. Given the planet, it is still necessary to add the impulse; so, to every creature nature added a little violence of direction in its proper path, a shove to put it on its way; in every instance, a slight generosity, a drop too much. Without electricity the air would rot, and without this violence of direction, which men and women have, without a spice of bigot and fanatic, no excitement, no efficiency. We aim above the mark, to hit the mark. Every act hath some falsehood of exaggeration in it. And when now and then comes along some sad, sharp-eyed man, who sees how paltry a game is played, and refuses to play, but blabs the secret;—how then? is the bird flown? O no, the wary Nature sends a new troop of fairer forms, of lordlier youths, with a little more excess of direction to hold them fast to their several aim; makes them a little wrongheaded in that direction in which they are rightest, and on goes the game again with new whirl, for a generation or two more. The child with his sweet pranks, the fool of his senses, commanded by every sight and sound, without any power to compare and rank his sensations, abandoned to a whistle or a painted chip, to a lead dragoon, or a gingerbread-dog, individualizing everything, generalizing nothing, delighted with every new thing, lies down at night overpowered by the fatigue, which this day of continual pretty madness has incurred. But Nature has answered her purpose with the curly, dimpled lunatic. She has tasked every faculty, and has secured the symmetrical growth of the bodily frame, by all these attitudes and exertions,—an end of the first importance, which could not be trusted to any care less perfect than her own. This glitter, this opaline lustre plays round the top of every toy to his eye, to ensure his fidelity, and he is deceived to his good. We are made alive and kept alive by the same arts. Let the stoics say what they please, we do not eat for the good of living, but because the meat is savory and the appetite is keen. The vegetable life does not content itself with casting from the flower or the tree a single seed, but it fills the air and earth with a prodigality of seeds, that, if thousands perish, thousands may plant themselves, that hundreds may come up, that tens may live to maturity, that, at least, one may replace the parent. All things betray the same calculated profusion. The excess of fear with which the animal frame is hedged round, shrinking from cold, starting at sight of a snake, or at a sudden noise, protects us, through a multitude of groundless alarms, from some one real danger at last. The lover seeks in marriage his private felicity and perfection, with no prospective end; and nature hides in his happiness her own end, namely, progeny, or the perpetuity of the race.

But the craft with which the world is made, runs also into the mind and character of men. No man is quite sane; each has a vein of folly in his composition, a slight determination of blood to the head, to make sure of holding him hard to some one point which nature had taken to heart. Great causes are never tried on their merits; but the cause is reduced to particulars to suit the size of the partizans, and the contention is ever hottest on minor matters. Not less remarkable is the overfaith of each man in the importance of what he has to do or say. The poet, the prophet, has a higher value for what he utters than any hearer, and therefore it gets spoken. The strong, self-complacent Luther declares with an emphasis, not to be mistaken, that "God himself cannot do without wise men." Jacob Behmen and George Fox betray their egotism in the pertinacity of their controversial tracts, and James Naylor once suffered himself to be worshipped as the Christ. Each prophet comes presently to identify himself with his thought, and to esteem his hat and shoes sacred. However this may discredit such persons with the judicious, it helps them with the people, as it gives heat, pungency, and publicity to their words. A similar experience is not infrequent in private life. Each young and ardent person writes a diary, in which, when the hours of prayer and penitence arrive, he inscribes his soul. The pages thus written are, to him, burning and fragrant: he reads them on his knees by midnight and by the morning star; he wets them with his tears: they are sacred; too good for the world, and hardly yet to be shown to the dearest friend. This is the man-child that is born to the soul, and her life still circulates in the babe. The umbilical cord has not yet been cut. After some time has elapsed, he begins to wish to admit his friend to this hallowed experience, and with hesitation, yet with firmness, exposes the pages to his eye. Will they not burn his eyes? The friend coldly turns them over, and passes from the writing to conversation, with easy transition, which strikes the other party with astonishment and vexation. He cannot suspect the writing itself.

Days and nights of fervid life, of communion with angels of darkness and of light, have engraved their shadowy characters on that tear-stained book. He suspects the intelligence or the heart of his friend. Is there then no friend? He cannot yet credit that one may have impressive experience, and yet may not know how to put his private fact into literature; and perhaps the discovery that wisdom has other tongues and ministers than we, that though we should hold our peace, the truth would not the less be spoken, might check injuriously the flames of our zeal. A man can only speak, so long as he does not feel his speech to be partial and inadequate. It is partial, but he does not see it to be so, whilst he utters it. As soon as he is released from the instinctive and particular, and sees its partiality, he shuts his mouth in disgust. For, no man can write anything, who does not think that what he writes is for the time the history of the world; or do anything well, who does not esteem his work to be of importance. My work may be of none, but I must not think it of none, or I shall not do it with impunity.

In like manner, there is throughout nature something mocking, something that leads us on and on, but arrives nowhere, keeps no faith with us. All promise outruns the performance. We live in a system of approximations. Every end is prospective of some other end, which is also temporary; a round and final success nowhere. We are encamped in nature, not domesticated. Hunger and thirst lead us on to eat and to drink; but bread and wine, mix and cook them how you will, leave us hungry and thirsty, after the stomach is full. It is the same with all our arts and performances. Our music, our poetry, our language itself are not satisfactions, but suggestions. The hunger for wealth, which reduces the planet to a garden, fools the eager pursuer. What is the end sought? Plainly to secure the ends of good sense and beauty, from the intrusion of deformity or vulgarity of any kind. But what an operose method! What a train of means to secure a little conversation! This palace of brick and stone, these servants, this kitchen, these stables, horses and equipage, this bank-stock, and file of mortgages; trade to all the world, country-house and cottage by the waterside, all for a little conversation, high, clear, and spiritual! Could it not be had as well by beggars on the highway? No, all these things came from successive efforts of these beggars to remove friction from the wheels of life, and give opportunity. Conversation, character, were the avowed ends; wealth was good as it appeased the animal cravings, cured the smoky chimney, silenced the creaking door, brought friends together in a warm and quiet room, and kept the children and the dinner-table in a different apartment. Thought, virtue, beauty, were the ends; but it was known that men of thought and virtue sometimes had the headache, or wet feet, or could lose good time whilst the room was getting warm in winter days. Unluckily, in the exertions necessary to remove these inconveniences, the main attention has been diverted to this object; the old aims have been lost sight of, and to remove friction has come to be the end. That is the ridicule of rich men, and Boston, London, Vienna, and now the governments generally of the world, are cities and governments of the rich, and the masses are not men, but poor men, that is, men who would be rich; this is the ridicule of the class, that they arrive with pains and sweat and fury nowhere; when all is done, it is for nothing. They are like one who has interrupted the conversation of a company to make his speech, and now has forgotten what he went to say. The appearance strikes the eye everywhere of an aimless society, of aimless nations. Were the ends of nature so great and cogent, as to exact this immense sacrifice of men?

Quite analogous to the deceits in life, there is, as might be expected, a similar effect on the eye from the face of external nature. There is in woods and waters a certain enticement and flattery, together with a failure to yield a present satisfaction. This disappointment is felt in every landscape. I have seen the softness and beauty of the summer-clouds floating feathery overhead, enjoying, as it seemed, their height and privilege of motion, whilst yet they appeared not so much the drapery of this place and hour, as forelooking to some pavilions and gardens of festivity beyond. It is an odd jealousy: but the poet finds himself not near enough to his object. The pine-tree, the river, the bank of flowers before him, does not seem to be nature. Nature is still elsewhere. This or this is but outskirt and far-off reflection and echo of the triumph that has passed by, and is now at its glancing splendor and heyday, perchance in the neighboring fields, or, if you stand in the field, then in the adjacent woods. The present object shall give you this sense of stillness that follows a pageant which has just gone by. What splendid distance, what recesses of ineffable pomp and loveliness in the sunset! But who can go where they are, or lay his hand or plant his foot thereon? Off they fall from the round world forever and ever. It is the same among the men and women, as among the silent trees; always a referred existence, an absence, never a presence and satisfaction. Is it, that beauty can never be grasped? in persons and in landscape is equally inaccessible? The accepted and betrothed lover has lost the wildest charm of his maiden in her acceptance of him. She was heaven whilst he pursued her as a star: she cannot be heaven, if she stoops to such a one as he.

What shall we say of this omnipresent appearance of that first projectile impulse, of this flattery and baulking of so many well-meaning creatures? Must we not suppose somewhere in the universe a slight treachery and derision? Are we not engaged to a serious resentment of this use that is made of us? Are we tickled trout, and fools of nature? One look at the face of heaven and earth lays all petulance at rest, and soothes us to wiser convictions. To the intelligent, nature converts itself into a vast promise, and will not be rashly explained. Her secret is untold. Many and many an Oedipus arrives: he has the whole mystery teeming in his brain. Alas! the same sorcery has spoiled his skill; no syllable can he shape on his lips. Her mighty orbit vaults like the fresh rainbow into the deep, but no archangel's wing was yet strong enough to follow it, and report of the return of the curve. But it also appears, that our actions are seconded and disposed to greater conclusions than we designed. We are escorted on every hand through life by spiritual agents, and a beneficent purpose lies in wait for us. We cannot bandy words with nature, or deal with her as we deal with persons. If we measure our individual forces against hers, we may easily feel as if we were the sport of an insuperable destiny. But if, instead of identifying ourselves with the work, we feel that the soul of the workman streams through us, we shall find the peace of the morning dwelling first in our hearts, and the fathomless powers of gravity and chemistry, and, over them, of life, preexisting within us in their highest form.

The uneasiness which the thought of our helplessness in the chain of causes occasions us, results from looking too much at one condition of nature, namely, Motion. But the drag is never taken from the wheel. Wherever the impulse exceeds, the Rest or Identity insinuates its compensation. All over the wide fields of earth grows the prunella or self-heal. After every foolish day we sleep off the fumes and furies of its hours; and though we are always engaged with particulars, and often enslaved to them, we bring with us to every experiment the innate universal laws. These, while they exist in the mind as ideas, stand around us in nature forever embodied, a present sanity to expose and cure the insanity of men. Our servitude to particulars betrays into a hundred foolish expectations. We anticipate a new era from the invention of a locomotive, or a balloon; the new engine brings with it the old checks. They say that by electromagnetism, your sallad shall be grown from the seed, whilst your fowl is roasting for dinner: it is a symbol of our modern aims and endeavors,—of our condensation and acceleration of objects: but nothing is gained: nature cannot be cheated: man's life is but seventy sallads long, grow they swift or grow they slow. In these checks and impossibilities, however, we find our advantage, not less than in the impulses. Let the victory fall where it will, we are on that side. And the knowledge that we traverse the whole scale of being, from the centre to the poles of nature, and have some stake in every possibility, lends that sublime lustre to death, which philosophy and religion have too outwardly and literally striven to express in the popular doctrine of the immortality of the soul. The reality is more excellent than the report. Here is no ruin, no discontinuity, no spent ball. The divine circulations never rest nor linger. Nature is the incarnation of a thought, and turns to a thought again, as ice becomes water and gas. The world is mind precipitated, and the volatile essence is forever escaping again into the state of free thought. Hence the virtue and pungency of the influence on the mind, of natural objects, whether inorganic or organized. Man imprisoned, man crystallized, man vegetative, speaks to man impersonated. That power which does not respect quantity, which makes the whole and the particle its equal channel, delegates its smile to the morning, and distils its essence into every drop of rain. Every moment instructs, and every object: for wisdom is infused into every form. It has been poured into us as blood; it convulsed us as pain; it slid into us as pleasure; it enveloped us in dull, melancholy days, or in days of cheerful labor; we did not guess its essence, until after a long time.

II

SPIRITUAL LAWS

When the act of reflection takes place in the mind, when we look at ourselves in the light of thought, we discover that our life is embosomed in beauty. Behind us, as we go, all things assume pleasing forms, as clouds do far off. Not only things familiar and stale, but even the tragic and terrible, are comely, as they take their place in the pictures of memory. The river-bank, the weed at the water-side, the old house, the foolish person,—however neglected in the passing,—have a grace in the past. Even the corpse that has lain in the chambers has added a solemn ornament to the house. The soul will not know either deformity or pain. If, in the hours of clear reason, we should speak the severest truth, we should say, that we had never made a sacrifice. In these hours the mind seems so great, that nothing can be taken from us that seems much. All loss, all pain, is particular; the universe remains to the heart unhurt. Neither vexations nor calamities abate our trust. No man ever stated his griefs as lightly as he might. Allow for exaggeration in the most patient and sorely ridden hack that ever was driven. For it is only the finite that has wrought and suffered; the infinite lies stretched in smiling repose.

The intellectual life may be kept clean and healthful, if man will live the life of nature, and not import into his mind difficulties which are none of his. No man need be perplexed in his speculations. Let him do and say what strictly belongs to him, and, though very ignorant of books, his nature shall not yield him any intellectual obstructions and doubts. Our young people are diseased with the theological problems of original sin, origin of evil, predestination, and the like. These never presented a practical difficulty to any man,—never darkened across any man's road, who did not go out of his way to seek them. These are the soul's mumps, and measles, and whooping-coughs, and those who have not caught them cannot describe their health or prescribe the cure. A simple mind will not know these enemies. It is quite another thing that he should be able to give account of his faith, and expound to another the theory of his self-union and freedom. This requires rare gifts. Yet, without this self-knowledge, there may be a sylvan strength and integrity in that which he is. "A few strong instincts and a few plain rules" suffice us.

My will never gave the images in my mind the rank they now take. The regular course of studies, the years of academial and professional education, have not yielded me better facts than some idle books under the bench at the Latin School. What we do not call education is more precious than that which we call so. We form no guess, at the time of receiving a thought, of its comparative value. And education often wastes its effort in attempts to thwart and balk this natural magnetism, which is sure to select what belongs to it.

In like manner, our moral nature is vitiated by any interference of our will. People represent virtue as a struggle, and take to themselves great airs upon their attainments, and the question is everywhere vexed, when a noble nature is commended, whether the man is not better who strives with temptation. But there is no merit in the matter. Either God is there, or he is not there. We love characters in proportion as they are impulsive and spontaneous. The less a man thinks or knows about his virtues, the better we like him. Timoleon's victories are the best victories; which ran and flowed like Homer's verses, Plutarch said. When we see a soul whose acts are all regal, graceful, and pleasant as roses, we must thank God that such things can be and are, and not turn sourly on the angel, and say, 'Crump is a better man with his grunting resistance to all his native devils.'

Not less conspicuous is the preponderance of nature over will in all practical life. There is less intention in history than we ascribe to it. We impute deep-laid, far-sighted plans to Caesar and Napoleon; but the best of their power was in nature, not in them. Men of an extraordinary success, in their honest moments, have always sung, 'Not unto us, not unto us.' According to the faith of their times, they have built altars to Fortune, or to Destiny, or to St. Julian. Their success lay in their parallelism to the course of thought, which found in them an unobstructed channel; and the wonders of which they were the visible conductors seemed to the eye their deed. Did the wires generate the galvanism? It is even true that there was less in them on which they could reflect, than in another; as the virtue of a pipe is to be smooth and hollow. That which externally seemed will and immovableness was willingness and self-annihilation. Could Shakespeare give a theory of Shakespeare? Could ever a man of prodigious mathematical genius convey to others any insight into his methods? If he could communicate that secret, it would instantly lose its exaggerated value, blending with the daylight and the vital energy the power to stand and to go.

The lesson is forcibly taught by these observations, that our life might be much easier and simpler than we make it; that the world might be a happier place than it is; that there is no need of struggles, convulsions, and despairs, of the wringing of the hands and the gnashing of the teeth; that we miscreate our own evils. We interfere with the optimism of nature; for, whenever we get this vantage-ground of the past, or of a wiser mind in the present, we are able to discern that we are begirt with laws which execute themselves.

The face of external nature teaches the same lesson. Nature will not have us fret and fume. She does not like our benevolence or our learning much better than she likes our frauds and wars. When we come out of the caucus, or the bank, or the Abolition-convention, or the Temperance-meeting, or the Transcendental club, into the fields and woods, she says to us, 'So hot? my little Sir.'

We are full of mechanical actions. We must needs intermeddle, and have things in our own way, until the sacrifices and virtues of society are odious. Love should make joy; but our benevolence is unhappy. Our Sunday-schools, and churches, and pauper-societies are yokes to the neck. We pain ourselves to please nobody. There are natural ways of arriving at the same ends at which these aim, but do not arrive. Why should all virtue work in one and the same way? Why should all give dollars? It is very inconvenient to us country folk, and we do not think any good will come of it. We have not dollars; merchants have; let them give them. Farmers will give corn; poets will sing; women will sew; laborers will lend a hand; the children will bring flowers. And why drag this dead weight of a Sunday-school over the whole Christendom? It is natural and beautiful that childhood should inquire, and maturity should teach; but it is time enough to answer questions when they are asked. Do not shut up the young people against their will in a pew, and force the children to ask them questions for an hour against their will.

If we look wider, things are all alike; laws, and letters, and creeds, and modes of living, seem a travestie of truth. Our society is encumbered by ponderous machinery, which resembles the endless aqueducts which the Romans built over hill and dale, and which are superseded by the discovery of the law that water rises to the level of its source. It is a Chinese wall which any nimble Tartar can leap over. It is a standing army, not so good as a peace. It is a graduated, titled, richly appointed empire, quite superfluous when town-meetings are found to answer just as well.

Let us draw a lesson from nature, which always works by short ways. When the fruit is ripe, it falls. When the fruit is despatched, the leaf falls. The circuit of the waters is mere falling. The walking of man and all animals is a falling forward. All our manual labor and works of strength, as prying, splitting, digging, rowing, and so forth, are done by dint of continual falling, and the globe, earth, moon, comet, sun, star, fall for ever and ever.

The simplicity of the universe is very different from the simplicity of a machine. He who sees moral nature out and out, and thoroughly knows how knowledge is acquired and character formed, is a pedant. The simplicity of nature is not that which may easily be read, but is inexhaustible. The last analysis can no wise be made. We judge of a man's wisdom by his hope, knowing that the perception of the inexhaustibleness of nature is an immortal youth. The wild fertility of nature is felt in comparing our rigid names and reputations with our fluid consciousness. We pass in the world for sects and schools, for erudition and piety, and we are all the time jejune babes. One sees very well how Pyrrhonism grew up. Every man sees that he is that middle point, whereof every thing may be affirmed and denied with equal reason. He is old, he is young, he is very wise, he is altogether ignorant. He hears and feels what you say of the seraphim, and of the tin-pedler. There is no permanent wise man, except in the figment of the Stoics. We side with the hero, as we read or paint, against the coward and the robber; but we have been ourselves that coward and robber, and shall be again, not in the low circumstance, but in comparison with the grandeurs possible to the soul.

A little consideration of what takes place around us every day would show us, that a higher law than that of our will regulates events; that our painful labors are unnecessary, and fruitless; that only

in our easy, simple, spontaneous action are we strong, and by content-
ing ourselves with obedience we become divine. Belief and love,—a
believing love will relieve us of a vast load of care. O my brothers,
God exists. There is a soul at the centre of nature, and over the will
of every man, so that none of us can wrong the universe. It has so
infused its strong enchantment into nature, that we prosper when we
accept its advice, and when we struggle to wound its creatures, our
hands are glued to our sides, or they beat our own breasts. The whole
course of things goes to teach us faith. We need only obey. There is
guidance for each of us, and by lowly listening we shall hear the right
word. Why need you choose so painfully your place, and occupation,
and associates, and modes of action, and of entertainment? Certainly
there is a possible right for you that precludes the need of balance
and wilful election. For you there is a reality, a fit place and congenial
duties. Place yourself in the middle of the stream of power and wisdom which animates all whom it floats, and you are without effort
impelled to truth, to right, and a perfect contentment. Then you put
all gainsayers in the wrong. Then you are the world, the measure of
right, of truth, of beauty. If we will not be mar-plots with our miserable interferences, the work, the society, letters, arts, science, religion
of men would go on far better than now, and the heaven predicted
from the beginning of the world, and still predicted from the bottom
of the heart, would organize itself, as do now the rose, and the air,
and the sun.

I say, *do not choose*; but that is a figure of speech by which I would
distinguish what is commonly called *choice* among men, and which is
a partial act, the choice of the hands, of the eyes, of the appetites, and
not a whole act of the man. But that which I call right or goodness is
the choice of my constitution; and that which I call heaven, and
inwardly aspire after, is the state or circumstance desirable to my constitution; and the action which I in all my years tend to do, is the
work for my faculties. We must hold a man amenable to reason for

the choice of his daily craft or profession. It is not an excuse any longer for his deeds, that they are the custom of his trade. What business has he with an evil trade? Has he not a *calling* in his character. Each man has his own vocation. The talent is the call. There is one direction in which all space is open to him. He has faculties silently inviting him thither to endless exertion. He is like a ship in a river; he runs against obstructions on every side but one; on that side all obstruction is taken away, and he sweeps serenely over a deepening channel into an infinite sea. This talent and this call depend on his organization, or the mode in which the general soul incarnates itself in him. He inclines to do something which is easy to him, and good when it is done, but which no other man can do. He has no rival. For the more truly he consults his own powers, the more difference will his work exhibit from the work of any other. His ambition is exactly proportioned to his powers. The height of the pinnacle is determined by the breadth of the base. Every man has this call of the power to do somewhat unique, and no man has any other call. The pretence that he has another call, a summons by name and personal election and outward "signs that mark him extraordinary, and not in the roll of common men," is fanaticism, and betrays obtuseness to perceive that there is one mind in all the individuals, and no respect of persons therein.

By doing his work, he makes the need felt which he can supply, and creates the taste by which he is enjoyed. By doing his own work, he unfolds himself. It is the vice of our public speaking that it has not abandonment. Somewhere, not only every orator but every man should let out all the length of all the reins; should find or make a frank and hearty expression of what force and meaning is in him. The common experience is, that the man fits himself as well as he can to the customary details of that work or trade he falls into, and tends it as a dog turns a spit. Then is he a part of the machine he moves; the man is lost. Until he can manage to communicate himself to others in his full stature and proportion, he does not yet find his vocation. He must find in that an outlet for his character, so that he may justify his work to their eyes. If the labor is mean, let him by his thinking and character make it liberal. Whatever he knows and thinks, whatever in his apprehension is worth doing, that let him communicate, or men will never know and honor him aright. Foolish, whenever you take the meanness and formality of that thing you do, instead of converting it into the obedient spiracle of your character and aims.

We like only such actions as have already long had the praise of men, and do not perceive that any thing man can do may be divinely done. We think greatness entailed or organized in some places or duties, in certain offices or occasions, and do not see that Paganini can extract rapture from a catgut, and Eulenstein from a jews-harp, and a nimble-fingered lad out of shreds of paper with his scissors, and Landseer out of swine, and the hero out of the pitiful habitation and company in which he was hidden. What we call obscure condition or vulgar society is that condition and society whose poetry is not yet written, but which you shall presently make as enviable and renowned as any. In our estimates, let us take a lesson from kings. The parts of hospitality, the connection of families, the impressiveness of death, and a thousand other things, royalty makes its own estimate of, and a royal mind will. To make habitually a new estimate,—that is elevation.

What a man does, that he has. What has he to do with hope or fear? In himself is his might. Let him regard no good as solid, but that which is in his nature, and which must grow out of him as long as he exists. The goods of fortune may come and go like summer leaves; let him scatter them on every wind as the momentary signs of his infinite productiveness.

He may have his own. A man's genius, the quality that differences him from every other, the susceptibility to one class of influences, the selection of what is fit for him, the rejection of what is unfit, determines for him the character of the universe. A man is a method, a progressive arrangement; a selecting principle, gathering his like to him, wherever he goes. He takes only his own out of the multiplicity that sweeps and circles round him. He is like one of those booms which are set out from the shore on rivers to catch drift-wood, or like the loadstone amongst splinters of steel. Those facts, words, persons, which dwell in his memory without his being able to say why, remain, because they have a relation to him not less real for being as yet unapprehended. They are symbols of value to him, as they can interpret parts of his consciousness which he would vainly seek words for in the conventional images of books and other minds. What attracts my attention shall have it, as I will go to the man who knocks at my door, whilst a thousand persons, as worthy, go by it, to whom I give no regard. It is enough that these particulars speak to me. A few anecdotes, a few traits of character, manners, face, a few incidents, have an emphasis in your memory out of all proportion to their apparent significance, if you measure them by the ordinary standards. They relate to your gift. Let them have their weight, and do not reject them, and cast about for illustration and facts more usual in literature. What your heart thinks great is great. The soul's emphasis is always right.

Over all things that are agreeable to his nature and genius, the man has the highest right. Everywhere he may take what belongs to his spiritual estate, nor can he take any thing else, though all doors were open, nor can all the force of men hinder him from taking so much. It is vain to attempt to keep a secret from one who has a right to know it. It will tell itself. That mood into which a friend can bring us is his dominion over us. To the thoughts of that state of mind he has a right. All the secrets of that state of mind he can compel. This is a law which statesmen use in practice. All the terrors of the French Republic, which held Austria in awe, were unable to command her diplomacy. But Napoleon sent to Vienna M. de Narbonne, one of the old noblesse, with the morals, manners, and name of that interest, saying, that it was indispensable to send to the old aristocracy of Europe men of the same connection, which, in fact, constitutes a sort of free-masonry. M. de Narbonne, in less than a fortnight, penetrated all the secrets of the imperial cabinet.

Nothing seems so easy as to speak and to be understood. Yet a man may come to find *that* the strongest of defenses and of ties,— that he has been understood; and he who has received an opinion may come to find it the most inconvenient of bonds.

If a teacher have any opinion which he wishes to conceal, his pupils will become as fully indoctrinated into that as into any which he publishes. If you pour water into a vessel twisted into coils and angles, it is vain to say, I will pour it only into this or that;—it will find its level in all. Men feel and act the consequences of your doctrine, without being able to show how they follow. Show us an arc of the curve, and a good mathematician will find out the whole figure. We are always reasoning from the seen to the unseen. Hence the perfect intelligence that subsists between wise men of remote ages. A man cannot bury his meanings so deep in his book, but time and like-minded men will find them. Plato had a secret doctrine, had he? What secret can he conceal from the eyes of Bacon? of Montaigne? of Kant? Therefore, Aristotle said of his works, "They are published and not published."

No man can learn what he has not preparation for learning, however near to his eyes is the object. A chemist may tell his most precious secrets to a carpenter, and he shall be never the wiser,—the secrets he would not utter to a chemist for an estate. God screens us evermore from premature ideas. Our eyes are holden that we cannot see things that stare us in the face, until the hour arrives when the mind is ripened; then we behold them, and the time when we saw them not is like a dream.

Not in nature but in man is all the beauty and worth he sees. The world is very empty, and is indebted to this gilding, exalting soul for all its pride. "Earth fills her lap with splendors" *not her own*. The vale of Tempe, Tivoli, and Rome are earth and water, rocks and sky. There are as good earth and water in a thousand places, yet how unaffecting!

People are not the better for the sun and moon, the horizon and the trees; as it is not observed that the keepers of Roman galleries, or the valets of painters, have any elevation of thought, or that librarians are wiser men than others. There are graces in the demeanour of a polished and noble person, which are lost upon the eye of a churl. These are like the stars whose light has not yet reached us.

He may see what he maketh. Our dreams are the sequel of our waking knowledge. The visions of the night bear some proportion to the visions of the day. Hideous dreams are exaggerations of the sins of the day. We see our evil affections embodied in bad physiognomies. On the Alps, the traveller sometimes beholds his own shadow magnified to a giant, so that every gesture of his hand is terrific. "My children," said an old man to his boys scared by a figure in the dark entry, "my children, you will never see any thing worse than yourselves." As in dreams, so in the scarcely less fluid events of the world, every man sees himself in colossal, without knowing that it is himself. The good, compared to the evil which he sees, is as his own good to his own evil. Every quality of his mind is magnified in some one acquaintance, and every emotion of his heart in some one. He is like a quincunx of trees, which counts five, east, west, north, or south; or, an initial, medial, and terminal acrostic. And why not? He cleaves to one person, and avoids another, according to their likeness or unlikeness to himself, truly seeking himself in his associates, and moreover in his trade, and habits, and gestures, and meats, and drinks; and comes at last to be faithfully represented by every view you take of his circumstances.

He may read what he writes. What can we see or acquire, but what we are? You have observed a skilful man reading Virgil. Well, that author is a thousand books to a thousand persons. Take the book into your two hands, and read your eyes out; you will never find what I find. If any ingenious reader would have a monopoly of the wisdom or delight he gets, he is as secure now the book is Englished, as if it were imprisoned in the Pelews' tongue. It is with a good book as it is with good company. Introduce a base person among gentlemen; it is all to no purpose; he is not their fellow. Every society protects itself. The company is perfectly safe, and he is not one of them, though his body is in the room.

What avails it to fight with the eternal laws of mind, which adjust the relation of all persons to each other, by the mathematical measure of their havings and beings? Gertrude is enamoured of Guy; how high, how aristocratic, how Roman his mien and manners! To live with him were life indeed, and no purchase is too great; and heaven and earth are moved to that end. Well, Gertrude has Guy; but what now avails how high, how aristocratic, how Roman his mien and manners, if his heart and aims are in the senate, in the theatre, and in the billiard-room, and she has no aims, no conversation, that can enchant her graceful lord?

He shall have his own society. We can love nothing but nature. The most wonderful talents, the most meritorious exertions, really avail very little with us; but nearness or likeness of nature,—how beautiful is the ease of its victory! Persons approach us famous for their beauty, for their accomplishments, worthy of all wonder for their charms and gifts; they dedicate their whole skill to the hour and the company, with very imperfect result. To be sure, it would be ungrateful in us not to praise them loudly. Then, when all is done, a person of related mind, a brother or sister by nature, comes to us so softly and easily, so nearly and intimately, as if it were the blood in our proper veins, that we feel as if some one was gone, instead of another having come; we are utterly relieved and refreshed; it is a sort of joyful solitude. We foolishly think in our days of sin, that we must court friends by compliance to the customs of society, to its dress, its breeding, and its estimates. But only that soul can be my friend which I encounter on the line of my own march, that soul to which I do not decline, and which does not decline to me, but, native of the same celestial latitude, repeats in its own all my experience. The scholar forgets himself, and apes the customs and costumes of the man of the world, to deserve the smile of beauty, and follows some giddy girl, not yet taught by religious passion to know the noble woman with all that is serene, oracular, and beautiful in her soul. Let him be great, and love shall follow him. Nothing is more deeply punished than the neglect of the affinities by which alone society should be formed, and the insane levity of choosing associates by others' eyes.

He may set his own rate. It is a maxim worthy of all acceptation, that a man may have that allowance he takes. Take the place and attitude which belong to you, and all men acquiesce. The world must be just. It leaves every man, with profound unconcern, to set his own rate. Hero or driveller, it meddles not in the matter. It will certainly accept your own measure of your doing and being, whether you sneak about and deny your own name, or whether you see your work produced to the concave sphere of the heavens, one with the revolution of the stars.

The same reality pervades all teaching. The man may teach by doing, and not otherwise. If he can communicate himself, he can teach, but not by words. He teaches who gives, and he learns who receives. There is no teaching until the pupil is brought into the same state or principle in which you are; a transfusion takes place; he is you, and you are he; then is a teaching; and by no unfriendly chance or bad company can he ever quite lose the benefit. But your propositions run out of one ear as they ran in at the other. We see it advertised that Mr. Grand will deliver an oration on the Fourth of July, and Mr. Hand before the Mechanics' Association, and we do not go thither, because we know that these gentlemen will not communicate their own character and experience to the company. If we had reason to expect such a confidence, we should go through all inconvenience and opposition. The sick would be carried in litters. But a public oration is an escapade, a non-committal, an apology, a gag, and not a communication, not a speech, not a man.

A like Nemesis presides over all intellectual works. We have yet to learn, that the thing uttered in words is not therefore affirmed. It must affirm itself, or no forms of logic or of oath can give it evidence. The sentence must also contain its own apology for being spoken.

The effect of any writing on the public mind is mathematically measurable by its depth of thought. How much water does it draw? If it awaken you to think, if it lift you from your feet with the great voice of eloquence, then the effect is to be wide, slow, permanent, over the minds of men; if the pages instruct you not, they will die like flies in the hour. The way to speak and write what shall not go out of fashion is, to speak and write sincerely. The argument which has not power to reach my own practice, I may well doubt, will fail to reach yours. But take Sidney's maxim:—"Look in thy heart and write." He that writes to himself writes to an eternal public. That statement only is fit to be made public, which you have come at in attempting to satisfy your own curiosity. The writer who takes his subject from his ear, and not from his heart, should know that he has lost as much as he seems to have gained, and when the empty book has gathered all its praise, and half the people say, 'What poetry! what genius!' it still needs fuel to make fire. That only profits which is profitable. Life alone can impart life; and though we should burst, we can only be valued as we make ourselves valuable. There is no luck in literary reputation. They who make up the final verdict upon every book are not the partial and noisy readers of the hour when it appears; but a court as of angels, a public not to be bribed, not to be entreated, and not to be overawed, decides upon every man's title to fame. Only those books come down which deserve to last. Gilt edges, vellum, and morocco, and presentation-copies to all the libraries, will not preserve a book in circulation beyond its intrinsic date. It must go with all Walpole's Noble and Royal Authors to its fate. Blackmore, Kotzebue, or Pollok may endure for a night, but Moses and Homer stand for ever. There are not in the world at any one time more than a dozen persons who read and understand Plato:—never enough to pay for an edition of his works; yet to every generation these come duly down, for the sake of those few persons, as if God brought them in his hand. "No book," said Bentley, "was ever written down by any but itself." The permanence of all books is fixed by no effort friendly or hostile, but by their own specific gravity, or the intrinsic importance of their contents to the constant mind of man. "Do not trouble yourself too much about the light on your statue," said Michel Angelo to the young sculptor; "the light of the public square will test its value."

In like manner the effect of every action is measured by the depth of the sentiment from which it proceeds. The great man knew not that he was great. It took a century or two for that fact to appear. What he did, he did because he must; it was the most natural thing in the world, and grew out of the circumstances of the moment. But now, every thing he did, even to the lifting of his finger or the eating of bread, looks large, all-related, and is called an institution.

These are the demonstrations in a few particulars of the genius of nature; they show the direction of the stream. But the stream is blood; every drop is alive. Truth has not single victories; all things are its organs,—not only dust and stones, but errors and lies. The laws of disease, physicians say, are as beautiful as the laws of health. Our philosophy is affirmative, and readily accepts the testimony of negative facts, as every shadow points to the sun. By a divine necessity, every fact in nature is constrained to offer its testimony.

Human character evermore publishes itself. The most fugitive deed and word, the mere air of doing a thing, the intimated purpose, expresses character. If you act, you show character; if you sit still, if you sleep, you show it. You think, because you have spoken nothing when others spoke, and have given no opinion on the times, on the church, on slavery, on marriage, on socialism, on secret societies, on the college, on parties and persons, that your verdict is still expected with curiosity as a reserved wisdom. Far otherwise; your silence answers very loud. You have no oracle to utter, and your fellow-men have learned that you cannot help them; for, oracles speak. Doth not wisdom cry, and understanding put forth her voice?

Dreadful limits are set in nature to the powers of dissimulation. Truth tyrannizes over the unwilling members of the body. Faces never lie, it is said. No man need be deceived, who will study the changes of expression. When a man speaks the truth in the spirit of truth, his eye is as clear as the heavens. When he has base ends, and speaks falsely, the eye is muddy and sometimes asquint.

I have heard an experienced counselor say, that he never feared the effect upon a jury of a lawyer who does not believe in his heart that his client ought to have a verdict. If he does not believe it, his unbelief will appear to the jury, despite all his protestations, and will become their unbelief. This is that law whereby a work of art, of whatever kind, sets us in the same state of mind wherein the artist was when he made it. That which we do not believe, we cannot adequately say, though we may repeat the words never so often. It was this conviction which Swedenborg expressed, when he described a group of persons in the spiritual world endeavouring in vain to articulate a proposition which they did not believe; but they could not, though they twisted and folded their lips even to indignation.

A man passes for that he is worth. Very idle is all curiosity concerning other people's estimate of us, and all fear of remaining unknown is not less so. If a man know that he can do any thing,—that he can do it better than any one else,—he has a pledge of the acknowledgment of that fact by all persons. The world is full of judgment-days, and into every assembly that a man enters, in every action he attempts, he is gauged and stamped. In every troop of boys that whoop and run in each yard and square, a new-comer is as well and accurately weighed in the course of a few days, and stamped with his right number, as if he had undergone a formal trial of his strength, speed, and temper. A stranger comes from a distant school, with better dress, with trinkets in his pockets, with airs and pretensions: an older boy says to himself, 'It's of no use; we shall find him out to-morrow.' 'What has he done?' is the divine question which searches men, and transpierces every false reputation. A fop may sit in any chair of the world, nor be distinguished for his hour from Homer and Washington; but there need never be any doubt concerning the respective ability of human beings. Pretension may sit still, but cannot act. Pretension never feigned an act of real greatness. Pretension never wrote an Iliad, nor drove back Xerxes, nor christianized the world, nor abolished slavery.

As much virtue as there is, so much appears; as much goodness as there is, so much reverence it commands. All the devils respect virtue. The high, the generous, the self-devoted sect will always instruct and command mankind. Never was a sincere word utterly lost. Never a magnanimity fell to the ground, but there is some heart to greet and accept it unexpectedly. A man passes for that he is worth. What he is engraves itself on his face, on his form, on his fortunes, in letters of light. Concealment avails him nothing; boasting nothing. There is confession in the glances of our eyes; in our smiles; in salutations; and the grasp of hands. His sin bedaubs him, mars all his good impression. Men know not why they do not trust him; but they do not trust him. His vice glasses his eye, cuts lines of mean expression in his cheek, pinches the nose, sets the mark of the beast on the back of the head, and writes O fool! fool! on the forehead of a king.

If you would not be known to do any thing, never do it. A man may play the fool in the drifts of a desert, but every grain of sand shall seem to see. He may be a solitary eater, but he cannot keep his foolish counsel. A broken complexion, a swinish look, ungenerous acts, and the want of due knowledge,—all blab. Can a cook, a Chiffinch, an Iachimo be mistaken for Zeno or Paul? Confucius exclaimed,—"How can a man be concealed! How can a man be concealed!"

On the other hand, the hero fears not, that, if he withhold the avowal of a just and brave act, it will go unwitnessed and unloved. One knows it,—himself,—and is pledged by it to sweetness of peace, and to nobleness of aim, which will prove in the end a better proclamation of it than the relating of the incident. Virtue is the adherence in action to the nature of things, and the nature of things makes it prevalent. It consists in a perpetual substitution of being for seeming, and with sublime propriety God is described as saying, I AM.

The lesson which these observations convey is, Be, and not seem. Let us acquiesce. Let us take our bloated nothingness out of the path of the divine circuits. Let us unlearn our wisdom of the world. Let us lie low in the Lord's power, and learn that truth alone makes rich and great.

If you visit your friend, why need you apologize for not having visited him, and waste his time and deface your own act? Visit him now. Let him feel that the highest love has come to see him, in thee, its lowest organ. Or why need you torment yourself and friend by secret self-reproaches that you have not assisted him or complimented him with gifts and salutations heretofore? Be a gift and a benediction. Shine with real light, and not with the borrowed reflection of gifts. Common men are apologies for men; they bow the head, excuse themselves with prolix reasons, and accumulate appearances, because the substance is not.

We are full of these superstitions of sense, the worship of magnitude. We call the poet inactive, because he is not a president, a merchant, or a porter. We adore an institution, and do not see that it is founded on a thought which we have. But real action is in silent moments. The epochs of our life are not in the visible facts of our choice of a calling, our marriage, our acquisition of an office, and the like, but in a silent thought by the way-side as we walk; in a thought which revises our entire manner of life, and says,—'Thus hast thou done, but it were better thus.' And all our after years, like menials, serve and wait on this, and, according to their ability, execute its will. This revisal or correction is a constant force, which, as a tendency, reaches through our lifetime. The object of the man, the aim of these moments, is to make daylight shine through him, to suffer the law to traverse his whole being without obstruction, so that, on what point soever of his doing your eye falls, it shall report truly of his character, whether it be his diet, his house, his religious forms, his society, his mirth, his vote, his opposition. Now he is not homogeneous, but heterogeneous, and the ray does not traverse; there are no thorough lights: but the eye of the beholder is puzzled, detecting many unlike tendencies, and a life not yet at one.

Why should we make it a point with our false modesty to disparage that man we are, and that form of being assigned to us? A good man is contented. I love and honor Epaminondas, but I do not wish to be Epaminondas. I hold it more just to love the world of this hour, than the world of his hour. Nor can you, if I am true, excite me to the least uneasiness by saying, 'He acted, and thou sittest still.' I see action to be good, when the need is, and sitting still to be also good. Epaminondas, if he was the man I take him for, would have sat still with joy and peace, if his lot had been mine. Heaven is large, and affords space for all modes of love and fortitude. Why should we be busybodies and superserviceable? Action and inaction are alike to the true. One piece of the tree is cut for a weathercock, and one for the sleeper of a bridge; the virtue of the wood is apparent in both.

I desire not to disgrace the soul. The fact that I am here certainly shows me that the soul had need of an organ here. Shall I not assume the post? Shall I skulk and dodge and duck with my unseasonable apologies and vain modesty, and imagine my being here impertinent? less pertinent than Epaminondas or Homer being there? and that the soul did not know its own needs? Besides, without any reasoning on the matter, I have no discontent. The good soul nourishes me, and unlocks new magazines of power and enjoyment to me every day. I will not meanly decline the immensity of good, because I have heard that it has come to others in another shape.

Besides, why should we be cowed by the name of Action? 'Tis a trick of the senses,—no more. We know that the ancestor of every action is a thought. The poor mind does not seem to itself to be any thing, unless it have an outside badge,—some Gentoo diet, or Quaker coat, or Calvinistic prayer-meeting, or philanthropic society, or a great donation, or a high office, or, any how, some wild contrasting action to testify that it is somewhat. The rich mind lies in the sun and sleeps, and is Nature. To think is to act.

Let us, if we must have great actions, make our own so. All action is of an infinite elasticity, and the least admits of being inflated with the celestial air until it eclipses the sun and moon. Let us seek one peace by fidelity. Let me heed my duties. Why need I go gadding into the scenes and philosophy of Greek and Italian history, before I have justified myself to my benefactors? How dare I read Washington's campaigns, when I have not answered the letters of my own correspondents? Is not that a just objection to much of our reading? It is a pusillanimous desertion of our work to gaze after our neighbours. It is peeping. Byron says of Jack Bunting,—

"He knew not what to say, and so he swore."

I may say it of our preposterous use of books,—He knew not what to do, and so *he read*. I can think of nothing to fill my time with, and I find the Life of Brant. It is a very extravagant compliment to pay to Brant, or to General Schuyler, or to General Washington. My time should be as good as their time,—my facts, my net of relations, as good as theirs, or either of theirs. Rather let me do my work so well that other idlers, if they choose, may compare my texture with the texture of these and find it identical with the best.

This over-estimate of the possibilities of Paul and Pericles, this under-estimate of our own, comes from a neglect of the fact of an identical nature. Bonaparte knew but one merit, and rewarded in one and the same way the good soldier, the good astronomer, the good poet, the good player. The poet uses the names of Caesar, of Tamerlane, of Bonduca, of Belisarius; the painter uses the conventional story of the Virgin Mary, of Paul, of Peter. He does not, therefore, defer to the nature of these accidental men, of these stock heroes. If the poet write a true drama, then he is Caesar, and not the player of Caesar; then the selfsame strain of thought, emotion as pure, wit as subtle, motions as swift, mounting, extravagant, and a heart as great, self-sufficing, dauntless, which on the waves of its love and hope can uplift all that is reckoned solid and precious in the world,—palaces, gardens, money, navies, kingdoms,—marking its own incomparable worth by the slight it casts on these gauds of men,—these all are his, and by the power of these he rouses the nations. Let a man believe in God, and not in names and places and persons. Let the great soul incarnated in some woman's form, poor and sad and single, in some Dolly or Joan, go out to service, and sweep chambers and scour floors, and its effulgent daybeams cannot be muffled or hid, but to sweep and scour will instantly appear supreme and beautiful actions, the top and radiance of human life, and all people will get mops and brooms; until, lo! suddenly the great soul has enshrined itself in some other form, and done some other deed, and that is now the flower and head of all living nature.

We are the photometers, we the irritable gold leaf and tinfoil that measure the accumulations of the subtle element. We know the authentic effects of the true fire through every one of its million disguises.

III
COMPENSATION

Ever since I was a boy, I have wished to write a discourse on Compensation: for it seemed to me when very young, that on this subject life was ahead of theology, and the people knew more than the preachers taught. The documents, too, from which the doctrine is to be drawn, charmed my fancy by their endless variety, and lay always before me, even in sleep; for they are the tools in our hands, the bread in our basket, the transactions of the street, the farm, and the dwelling-house, greetings, relations, debts and credits, the influence of character, the nature and endowment of all men. It seemed to me, also, that in it might be shown men a ray of divinity, the present action of the soul of this world, clean from all vestige of tradition, and so the heart of man might be bathed by an inundation of eternal love, conversing with that which he knows was always and always must be, because it really is now. It appeared, moreover, that if this doctrine could be stated in terms with any resemblance to those bright intuitions in which this truth is sometimes revealed to us, it would be a star in many dark hours and crooked passages in our journey that would not suffer us to lose our way.

I was lately confirmed in these desires by hearing a sermon at church. The preacher, a man esteemed for his orthodoxy, unfolded in the ordinary manner the doctrine of the Last Judgment. He assumed, that judgment is not executed in this world; that the wicked are successful; that the good are miserable; and then urged from reason and from Scripture a compensation to be made to both parties in the next life. No offence appeared to be taken by the congregation at this doctrine. As far as I could observe, when the meeting broke up, they separated without remark on the sermon.

Yet what was the import of this teaching? What did the preacher mean by saying that the good are miserable in the present life? Was it that houses and lands, offices, wine, horses, dress, luxury, are had by unprincipled men, whilst the saints are poor and despised; and that a compensation is to be made to these last hereafter, by giving them the like gratifications another day,— bank-stock and doubloons, venison and champagne? This must be the compensation intended; for what else? Is it that they are to have leave to pray and praise? to love and serve men? Why, that they can do now. The legitimate inference the disciple would draw was,— 'We are to have such a good time as the sinners have now';—or, to push it to its extreme import,—'You sin now; we shall sin by and by; we would sin now, if we could; not being successful, we expect our revenge to-morrow.'

The fallacy lay in the immense concession, that the bad are successful; that justice is not done now. The blindness of the preacher consisted in deferring to the base estimate of the market of what constitutes a manly success, instead of confronting and convicting the world from the truth; announcing the presence of the soul; the omnipotence of the will: and so establishing the standard of good and ill, of success and falsehood.

I find a similar base tone in the popular religious works of the day, and the same doctrines assumed by the literary men when occasionally they treat the related topics. I think that our popular theology has gained in decorum, and not in principle, over the superstitions it has displaced. But men are better than this theology. Their daily life gives it the lie. Every ingenuous and aspiring soul leaves the doctrine behind him in his own experience; and all men feel sometimes the falsehood which they cannot demonstrate. For men are wiser than they know. That which they hear in schools and pulpits without after-thought, if said in conversation, would probably be questioned in silence. If a man dogmatize in a mixed company on Providence and the divine laws, he is answered by a silence which conveys well enough to an observer the dissatisfaction of the hearer, but his incapacity to make his own statement.

I shall attempt in this and the following chapter to record some facts that indicate the path of the law of Compensation; happy beyond my expectation, if I shall truly draw the smallest arc of this circle.

POLARITY, or action and reaction, we meet in every part of nature; in darkness and light; in heat and cold; in the ebb and flow of waters; in male and female; in the inspiration and expiration of plants and animals; in the equation of quantity and quality in the fluids of the animal body; in the systole and diastole of the heart; in the undulations of fluids, and of sound; in the centrifugal and centripetal gravity; in electricity, galvanism, and chemical affinity. Superinduce magnetism at one end of a needle; the opposite magnetism takes place at the other end. If the south attracts, the north repels. To empty here, you must condense there. An inevitable dualism bisects nature, so that each thing is a half, and suggests another thing to make it whole; as, spirit, matter; man, woman; odd, even; subjective, objective; in, out; upper, under; motion, rest; yea, nay.

Whilst the world is thus dual, so is every one of its parts. The entire system of things gets represented in every particle. There is somewhat that resembles the ebb and flow of the sea, day and night, man and woman, in a single needle of the pine, in a kernel of corn, in each individual of every animal tribe. The reaction, so grand in the elements, is repeated within these small boundaries. For example, in the animal kingdom the physiologist has observed that no creatures are favorites, but a certain compensation balances every gift and every defect. A surplusage given to one part is paid out of a reduction from another part of the same creature. If the head and neck are enlarged, the trunk and extremities are cut short.

The theory of the mechanic forces is another example. What we gain in power is lost in time; and the converse. The periodic or compensating errors of the planets is another instance. The influences of climate and soil in political history are another. The cold climate invigorates. The barren soil does not breed fevers, crocodiles, tigers, or scorpions.

The same dualism underlies the nature and condition of man. Every excess causes a defect; every defect an excess. Every sweet hath its sour; every evil its good. Every faculty which is a receiver of pleasure has an equal penalty put on its abuse. It is to answer for its moderation with its life. For every grain of wit there is a grain of folly. For every thing you have missed, you have gained something else; and for every thing you gain, you lose something. If riches increase, they are increased that use them. If the gatherer gathers too much, nature takes out of the man what she puts into his chest; swells the estate, but kills the owner. Nature hates monopolies and exceptions. The waves of the sea do not more speedily seek a level from their loftiest tossing, than the varieties of condition tend to equalize themselves. There is always some levelling circumstance that puts down the overbearing, the strong, the rich, the fortunate, substantially on the same ground with all others. Is a man too strong and fierce for society, and by temper and position a bad citizen,—a morose ruffian, with a dash of the pirate in him;— nature sends him a troop of pretty sons and daughters, who are getting along in the dame's classes at the village school, and love and fear for them smoothes his grim scowl to courtesy. Thus she contrives to intenerate the granite and felspar, takes the boar out and puts the lamb in, and keeps her balance true.

The farmer imagines power and place are fine things. But the President has paid dear for his White House. It has commonly cost him all his peace, and the best of his manly attributes. To preserve for a short time so conspicuous an appearance before the world, he is content to eat dust before the real masters who stand erect behind the throne. Or, do men desire the more substantial and permanent grandeur of genius? Neither has this an immunity. He who by force of will or of thought is great, and overlooks thousands, has the charges of that eminence. With every influx of light comes new danger. Has he light? he must bear witness to the light, and always outrun that sympathy which gives him such keen satisfaction, by his fidelity to new revelations of the incessant soul. He must hate father and mother, wife and child. Has he all that the world loves and admires and covets?—he must cast behind him their admiration, and afflict them by faithfulness to his truth, and become a byword and a hissing.

This law writes the laws of cities and nations. It is in vain to build or plot or combine against it. Things refuse to be mismanaged long: *Res nolunt diu male administrari.* Though no checks to a new evil appear, the checks exist, and will appear. If the government is cruel, the governor's life is not safe. If you tax too high, the revenue will yield nothing. If you make the criminal code sanguinary, juries will not convict. If the law is too mild, private vengeance comes in. If the government is a terrific democracy, the pressure is resisted by an overcharge of energy in the citizen, and life glows with a fiercer flame. The true life and satisfactions of man seem to elude the utmost rigors or felicities of condition, and to establish themselves with great indifference under all varieties of circumstances. Under all governments the influence of character remains the same,—in Turkey and in

New England about alike. Under the primeval despots of Egypt, history honestly confesses that man must have been as free as culture could make him.

These appearances indicate the fact that the universe is represented in every one of its particles. Every thing in nature contains all the powers of nature. Every thing is made of one hidden stuff; as the naturalist sees one type under every metamorphosis, and regards a horse as a running man, a fish as a swimming man, a bird as a flying man, a tree as a rooted man. Each new form repeats not only the main character of the type, but part for part all the details, all the aims, furtherances, hindrances, energies, and whole system of every other. Every occupation, trade, art, transaction, is a compend of the world, and a correlative of every other. Each one is an entire emblem of human life; of its good and ill, its trials, its enemies, its course and its end. And each one must somehow accommodate the whole man, and recite all his destiny.

The world globes itself in a drop of dew. The microscope cannot find the animalcule which is less perfect for being little. Eyes, ears, taste, smell, motion, resistance, appetite, and organs of reproduction that take hold on eternity,—all find room to consist in the small creature. So do we put our life into every act. The true doctrine of omnipresence is, that God reappears with all his parts in every moss and cobweb. The value of the universe contrives to throw itself into every point. If the good is there, so is the evil; if the affinity, so the repulsion; if the force, so the limitation.

Thus is the universe alive. All things are moral. That soul, which within us is a sentiment, outside of us is a law. We feel its inspiration; out there in history we can see its fatal strength. "It is in the world, and the world was made by it." Justice is not postponed. A perfect equity adjusts its balance in all parts of life. { *Oi chusoi Dios aei enpiptousi*},—The dice of God are always loaded. The world looks like a multiplication-table, or a mathematical equation, which, turn it how you will, balances itself. Take what figure you will, its exact value, nor more nor less, still returns to you. Every secret is told, every crime is punished, every virtue rewarded, every wrong redressed, in silence and certainty. What we call retribution is the universal necessity by which the whole appears wherever a part appears. If you see smoke, there must be fire. If you see a hand or a limb, you know that the trunk to which it belongs is there behind.

Every act rewards itself, or, in other words, integrates itself, in a twofold manner; first, in the thing, or in real nature; and secondly, in the circumstance, or in apparent nature. Men call the circumstance the retribution. The causal retribution is in the thing, and is seen by the soul. The retribution in the circumstance is seen by the understanding; it is inseparable from the thing, but is often spread over a long time, and so does not become distinct until after many years. The specific stripes may follow late after the offence, but they follow because they accompany it. Crime and punishment grow out of one stem. Punishment is a fruit that unsuspected ripens within the flower of the pleasure which concealed it. Cause and effect, means and ends, seed and fruit, cannot be severed; for the effect already blooms in the cause, the end preexists in the means, the fruit in the seed.

Whilst thus the world will be whole, and refuses to be disparted, we seek to act partially, to sunder, to appropriate; for example,—to gratify the senses, we sever the pleasure of the senses from the needs of the character. The ingenuity of man has always been dedicated to the solution of one problem,—how to detach the sensual sweet, the sensual strong, the sensual bright, &c., from the moral sweet, the moral deep, the moral fair; that is, again, to contrive to cut clean off this upper surface so thin as to leave it bottomless; to get a *one end*, without an *other end*. The soul says, Eat; the body would feast. The soul says, The man and woman shall be one flesh and one soul; the body would join the flesh only. The soul says, Have dominion over all things to the ends of virtue; the body would have the power over things to its own ends.

The soul strives amain to live and work through all things. It would be the only fact. All things shall be added unto it power, pleasure, knowledge, beauty. The particular man aims to be somebody; to set up for himself; to truck and higgle for a private good; and, in particulars, to ride, that he may ride; to dress, that he may be dressed; to eat, that he may eat; and to govern, that he may be seen. Men seek to be great; they would have offices, wealth, power, and fame. They think that to be great is to possess one side of nature,—the sweet, without the other side,—the bitter.

This dividing and detaching is steadily counteracted. Up to this day, it must be owned, no projector has had the smallest success. The parted water reunites behind our hand. Pleasure is taken out of pleasant things, profit out of profitable things, power out of strong things, as soon as we seek to separate them from the whole. We can no more halve things and get the sensual good, by itself, than we can get an inside that shall have no outside, or a light without a shadow. "Drive out nature with a fork, she comes running back."

Life invests itself with inevitable conditions, which the unwise seek to dodge, which one and another brags that he does not know; that they do not touch him;—but the brag is on his lips, the conditions are in his soul. If he escapes them in one part, they attack him in another more vital part. If he has escaped them in form, and in the appearance, it is because he has resisted his life, and fled from himself, and the retribution is so much death. So signal is the failure of all attempts to make this separation of the good from the tax, that the experiment would not be tried,—since to try it is to be mad,—but for the circumstance, that when the disease began in the will, of rebellion and separation, the intellect is at once infected, so that the man ceases to see God whole in each object, but is able to see the sensual allurement of an object, and not see the sensual hurt; he sees the mermaid's head, but not the dragon's tail; and thinks he can cut off that which he would have, from that which he would not have. "How secret art thou who dwellest in the highest heavens in silence, O thou only great God, sprinkling with an unwearied Providence certain penal blindnesses upon such as have unbridled desires!"

The human soul is true to these facts in the painting of fable, of history, of law, of proverbs, of conversation. It finds a tongue in literature unawares. Thus the Greeks called Jupiter, Supreme Mind; but having traditionally ascribed to him many base actions, they involuntarily made amends to reason, by tying up the hands of so bad a god. He is made as helpless as a king of England. Prometheus knows one secret which Jove must bargain for; Minerva, another. He cannot get his own thunders; Minerva keeps the key of them.

> *"Of all the gods, I only know the keys*
> *That ope the solid doors within whose vaults*
> *His thunders sleep."*

A plain confession of the in-working of the All, and of its moral aim. The Indian mythology ends in the same ethics; and it would seem impossible for any fable to be invented and get any currency which was not moral. Aurora forgot to ask youth for her lover, and though Tithonus is immortal, he is old. Achilles is not quite invulnerable; the sacred waters did not wash the heel by which Thetis held him. Siegfried, in the Nibelungen, is not quite immortal, for a leaf fell on his back whilst he was bathing in the dragon's blood, and that spot which it covered is mortal. And so it must be. There is a crack in every thing God has made. It would seem, there is always this vindictive circumstance stealing in at unawares, even into the wild poesy in which the human fancy attempted to make bold holiday, and to shake itself free of the old laws,—this back-stroke, this kick of the gun, certifying that the law is fatal; that in nature nothing can be given, all things are sold.

This is that ancient doctrine of Nemesis, who keeps watch in the universe, and lets no offence go unchastised. The Furies, they said, are attendants on justice, and if the sun in heaven should transgress his path, they would punish him. The poets related that stone walls, and iron swords, and leathern thongs had an occult sympathy with the wrongs of their owners; that the belt which Ajax gave Hector dragged the Trojan hero over the field at the wheels of the car of Achilles, and the sword which Hector gave Ajax was that on whose point Ajax fell. They recorded, that when the Thasians erected a statue to Theagenes, a victor in the games, one of his rivals went to it by night, and endeavoured to throw it down by repeated blows, until at last he moved it from its pedestal, and was crushed to death beneath its fall.

This voice of fable has in it somewhat divine. It came from thought above the will of the writer. That is the best part of each writer, which has nothing private in it; that which he does not know; that which flowed out of his constitution, and not from his too active invention; that which in the study of a single artist you might not easily find, but in the study of many, you would abstract as the spirit of them all. Phidias it is not, but the work of man in that early Hellenic world, that I would know. The name and circumstance of Phidias, however convenient for history, embarrass when we come to the highest criticism. We are to see that which man was tending to do in a given period, and was hindered, or, if you will, modified in doing, by the interfering volitions of Phidias, of Dante, of Shakespeare, the organ whereby man at the moment wrought.

Still more striking is the expression of this fact in the proverbs of all nations, which are always the literature of reason, or the statements of an absolute truth, without qualification. Proverbs, like the sacred books of each nation, are the sanctuary of the intuitions. That which the droning world, chained to appearances, will not allow the realist to say in his own words, it will suffer him to say in proverbs without contradiction. And this law of laws which the pulpit, the senate, and the college deny, is hourly preached in all markets and workshops by flights of proverbs, whose teaching is as true and as omnipresent as that of birds and flies.

All things are double, one against another.—Tit for tat; an eye for an eye; a tooth for a tooth; blood for blood; measure for measure; love for love.—Give and it shall be given you.—He that watereth shall be watered himself.—What will you have? quoth God; pay for it and take it.—Nothing venture, nothing have.—Thou shalt be paid exactly for what thou hast done, no more, no less.—Who doth not work shall not eat.—Harm watch, harm catch.—Curses always recoil on the head of him who imprecates them.—If you put a chain around the neck of a slave, the other end fastens itself around your own.—Bad counsel confounds the adviser.—The Devil is an ass.

It is thus written, because it is thus in life. Our action is overmastered and characterized above our will by the law of nature. We aim at a petty end quite aside from the public good, but our act arranges itself by irresistible magnetism in a line with the poles of the world.

A man cannot speak but he judges himself. With his will, or against his will, he draws his portrait to the eye of his companions by every word. Every opinion reacts on him who utters it. It is a threadball thrown at a mark, but the other end remains in the thrower's bag. Or, rather, it is a harpoon hurled at the whale, unwinding, as it flies, a coil of cord in the boat, and if the harpoon is not good, or not well thrown, it will go nigh to cut the steersman in twain, or to sink the boat.

You cannot do wrong without suffering wrong. "No man had ever a point of pride that was not injurious to him," said Burke. The exclusive in fashionable life does not see that he excludes himself from enjoyment, in the attempt to appropriate it. The exclusionist in religion does not see that he shuts the door of heaven on himself, in striving to shut out others. Treat men as pawns and ninepins, and you shall suffer as well as they. If you leave out their heart, you shall lose your own. The senses would make things of all persons; of women, of children, of the poor. The vulgar proverb, "I will get it from his purse or get it from his skin," is sound philosophy.

All infractions of love and equity in our social relations are speedily punished. They are punished by fear. Whilst I stand in simple relations to my fellow-man, I have no displeasure in meeting him. We meet as water meets water, or as two currents of air mix, with perfect diffusion and interpenetration of nature. But as soon as there is any departure from simplicity, and attempt at halfness, or good for me that is not good for him, my neighbour feels the wrong; he shrinks from me as far as I have shrunk from him; his eyes no longer seek mine; there is war between us; there is hate in him and fear in me.

All the old abuses in society, universal and particular, all unjust accumulations of property and power, are avenged in the same manner. Fear is an instructer of great sagacity, and the herald of all revolutions. One thing he teaches, that there is rottenness where he appears. He is a carrion crow, and though you see not well what he hovers for, there is death somewhere. Our property is timid, our laws are timid, our cultivated classes are timid. Fear for ages has boded and mowed and gibbered over government and property. That obscene bird is not there for nothing. He indicates great wrongs which must be revised.

Of the like nature is that expectation of change which instantly follows the suspension of our voluntary activity. The terror of cloudless noon, the emerald of Polycrates, the awe of prosperity, the instinct which leads every generous soul to impose on itself tasks of a noble asceticism and vicarious virtue, are the tremblings of the balance of justice through the heart and mind of man.

Experienced men of the world know very well that it is best to pay scot and lot as they go along, and that a man often pays dear for a small frugality. The borrower runs in his own debt. Has a man gained any thing who has received a hundred favors and rendered none? Has he gained by borrowing, through indolence or cunning, his neighbour's wares, or horses, or money? There arises on the deed the instant acknowledgment of benefit on the one part, and of debt on the other; that is, of superiority and inferiority. The transaction remains in the memory of himself and his neighbour; and every new transaction alters, according to its nature, their relation to each other. He may soon come to see that he had better have broken his own bones than to have ridden in his neighbour's coach, and that "the highest price he can pay for a thing is to ask for it."

A wise man will extend this lesson to all parts of life, and know that it is the part of prudence to face every claimant, and pay every just demand on your time, your talents, or your heart. Always pay; for, first or last, you must pay your entire debt. Persons and events may stand for a time between you and justice, but it is only a postponement. You must pay at last your own debt. If you are wise, you will dread a prosperity which only loads you with more. Benefit is the end of nature. But for every benefit which you receive, a tax is levied. He is great who confers the most benefits. He is base—and that is the one base thing in the universe—to receive favors and render none. In the order of nature we cannot render benefits to those from whom we receive them, or only seldom. But the benefit we receive must be rendered again, line for line, deed for deed, cent for cent, to somebody. Beware of too much good staying in your hand. It will fast corrupt and worm worms. Pay it away quickly in some sort.

Labor is watched over by the same pitiless laws. Cheapest, say the prudent, is the dearest labor. What we buy in a broom, a mat, a wagon, a knife, is some application of good sense to a common want. It is best to pay in your land a skilful gardener, or to buy good sense applied to gardening; in your sailor, good sense applied to navigation; in the house, good sense applied to cooking, sewing, serving; in your agent, good sense applied to accounts and affairs. So do you multiply your presence, or spread yourself throughout your estate. But because of the dual constitution of things, in labor as in life there can be no cheating. The thief steals from himself. The swindler swindles himself. For the real price of labor is knowledge and virtue, whereof wealth and credit are signs. These signs, like paper money, may be counterfeited or stolen, but that which they represent, namely, knowledge and virtue, cannot be counterfeited or stolen. These ends of labor cannot be answered but by real exertions of the mind, and in obedience to pure motives. The cheat, the defaulter, the gambler, cannot extort the knowledge of material and moral nature which his honest care and pains yield to the operative. The law of nature is, Do the thing, and you shall have the power: but they who do not the thing have not the power.

Human labor, through all its forms, from the sharpening of a stake to the construction of a city or an epic, is one immense illustration of the perfect compensation of the universe. The absolute balance of Give and Take, the doctrine that every thing has its price,—and if that price is not paid, not that thing but something else is obtained, and that it is impossible to get any thing without its price,—is not less sublime in the columns of a leger than in the budgets of states, in the laws of light and darkness, in all the action and reaction of nature. I cannot doubt that the high laws which each man sees implicated in those processes with which he is conversant, the stern ethics which sparkle on his chisel-edge, which are measured out by his plumb and foot-rule, which stand as manifest in the footing of the shop-bill as in the history of a state,—do recommend to him his trade, and though seldom named, exalt his business to his imagination.

The league between virtue and nature engages all things to assume a hostile front to vice. The beautiful laws and substances of the world persecute and whip the traitor. He finds that things are arranged for truth and benefit, but there is no den in the wide world to hide a rogue. Commit a crime, and the earth is made of glass. Commit a crime, and it seems as if a coat of snow fell on the ground, such as reveals in the woods the track of every partridge and fox and squirrel and mole. You cannot recall the spoken word, you cannot wipe out the foot-track, you cannot draw up the ladder, so as to leave no inlet or clew. Some damning circumstance always transpires. The laws and substances of nature—water, snow, wind, gravitation—become penalties to the thief.

On the other hand, the law holds with equal sureness for all right action. Love, and you shall be loved. All love is mathematically just, as much as the two sides of an algebraic equation. The good man has absolute good, which like fire turns every thing to its own nature, so that you cannot do him any harm; but as the royal armies sent against Napoleon, when he approached, cast down their colors and from enemies became friends, so disasters of all kinds, as sickness, offence, poverty, prove benefactors:—

"Winds blow and waters roll
Strength to the brave, and power and deity,
Yet in themselves are nothing."

The good are befriended even by weakness and defect. As no man had ever a point of pride that was not injurious to him, so no man had ever a defect that was not somewhere made useful to him. The stag in the fable admired his horns and blamed his feet, but when the hunter came, his feet saved him, and afterwards, caught in the thicket, his horns destroyed him. Every man in his lifetime needs to thank his faults. As no man thoroughly understands a truth until he has contended against it, so no man has a thorough acquaintance with the hindrances or talents of men, until he has suffered from the one, and seen the triumph of the other over his own want of the same. Has he a defect of temper that unfits him to live in society? Thereby he is driven to entertain himself alone, and acquire habits of self-help; and thus, like the wounded oyster, he mends his shell with pearl.

Our strength grows out of our weakness. The indignation which arms itself with secret forces does not awaken until we are pricked and stung and sorely assailed. A great man is always willing to be little. Whilst he sits on the cushion of advantages, he goes to sleep. When he is pushed, tormented, defeated, he has a chance to learn something; he has been put on his wits, on his manhood; he has gained facts; learns his ignorance; is cured of the insanity of conceit; has got moderation and real skill. The wise man throws himself on the side of his assailants. It is more his interest than it is theirs to find his weak point. The wound cicatrizes and falls off from him like a dead skin, and when they would triumph, lo! he has passed on invulnerable. Blame is safer than praise. I hate to be defended in a newspaper. As long as all that is said is said against me, I feel a certain assurance of success. But as soon as honeyed words of praise are spoken for me, I feel as one that lies unprotected before his enemies. In general, every evil to which we do not succumb is a benefactor. As the Sandwich Islander believes that the strength and valor of the enemy he kills passes into himself, so we gain the strength of the temptation we resist.

The same guards which protect us from disaster, defect, and enmity, defend us, if we will, from selfishness and fraud. Bolts and bars are not the best of our institutions, nor is shrewdness in trade a mark of wisdom. Men suffer all their life long, under the foolish superstition that they can be cheated. But it is as impossible for a man to be cheated by any one but himself, as for a thing to be and not to be at the same time. There is a third silent party to all our bargains. The nature and soul of things takes on itself the guaranty of the fulfillment of every contract, so that honest service cannot come to loss. If you serve an ungrateful master, serve him the more. Put God in your debt. Every stroke shall be repaid. The longer the payment is withholden, the better for you; for compound interest on compound interest is the rate and usage of this exchequer.

The history of persecution is a history of endeavours to cheat nature, to make water run up hill, to twist a rope of sand. It makes no difference whether the actors be many or one, a tyrant or a mob. A mob is a society of bodies voluntarily bereaving themselves of reason, and traversing its work. The mob is man voluntarily descending to the nature of the beast. Its fit hour of activity is night. Its actions are insane like its whole constitution. It persecutes a principle; it would whip a right; it would tar and feather justice, by inflicting fire and outrage upon the houses and persons of those who have these. It resembles the prank of boys, who run with fire-engines to put out the ruddy aurora streaming to the stars. The inviolate spirit turns their spite against the wrongdoers. The martyr cannot be dishonored. Every lash inflicted is a tongue of fame; every prison, a more illustrious abode; every burned book or house enlightens the world; every suppressed or expunged word reverberates through the earth from side to side. Hours of sanity and consideration are always arriving to communities, as to individuals, when the truth is seen, and the martyrs are justified.

Thus do all things preach the indifferency of circumstances. The man is all. Every thing has two sides, a good and an evil. Every advantage has its tax. I learn to be content. But the doctrine of compensation is not the doctrine of indifferency. The thoughtless say, on hearing these representations,—What boots it to do well? there is one event to good and evil; if I gain any good, I must pay for it; if I lose any good, I gain some other; all actions are indifferent.

There is a deeper fact in the soul than compensation, to wit, its own nature. The soul is not a compensation, but a life. The soul *is*. Under all this running sea of circumstance, whose waters ebb and flow with perfect balance, lies the aboriginal abyss of real Being. Essence, or God, is not a relation, or a part, but the whole. Being is the vast affirmative, excluding negation, self-balanced, and swallowing up all relations, parts, and times within itself. Nature, truth, virtue, are the influx from thence. Vice is the absence or departure of the same. Nothing, Falsehood, may indeed stand as the great Night or shade, on which, as a background, the living universe paints itself forth; but no fact is begotten by it; it cannot work; for it is not. It cannot work any good; it cannot work any harm. It is harm inasmuch as it is worse not to be than to be.

We feel defrauded of the retribution due to evil acts, because the criminal adheres to his vice and contumacy, and does not come to a crisis or judgment anywhere in visible nature. There is no stunning confutation of his nonsense before men and angels. Has he therefore outwitted the law? Inasmuch as he carries the malignity and the lie with him, he so far deceases from nature. In some manner there will be a demonstration of the wrong to the understanding also; but should we not see it, this deadly deduction makes square the eternal account.

Neither can it be said, on the other hand, that the gain of rectitude must be bought by any loss. There is no penalty to virtue; no penalty to wisdom; they are proper additions of being. In a virtuous action, I properly *am*; in a virtuous act, I add to the world; I plant into deserts conquered from Chaos and Nothing, and see the darkness receding on the limits of the horizon. There can be no excess to love; none to knowledge; none to beauty, when these attributes are considered in the purest sense. The soul refuses limits, and always affirms an Optimism, never a Pessimism.

His life is a progress, and not a station. His instinct is trust. Our instinct uses "more" and "less" in application to man, of the *presence of the soul*, and not of its absence; the brave man is greater than the coward; the true, the benevolent, the wise, is more a man, and not less, than the fool and knave. There is no tax on the good of virtue; for that is the incoming of God himself, or absolute existence, without any comparative. Material good has its tax, and if it came without desert or sweat, has no root in me, and the next wind will blow it away. But all the good of nature is the soul's, and may be had, if paid for in nature's lawful coin, that is, by labor which the heart and the head allow. I no longer wish to meet a good I do not earn, for example, to find a pot of buried gold, knowing that it brings with it new burdens. I do not wish more external goods,—neither possessions, nor honors, nor powers, nor persons. The gain is apparent; the tax is certain. But there is no tax on the knowledge that the compensation exists, and that it is not desirable to dig up treasure. Herein I rejoice with a serene eternal peace. I contract the boundaries of possible mischief. I learn the wisdom of St. Bernard,—"Nothing can work me damage except myself; the harm that I sustain I carry about with me, and never am a real sufferer but by my own fault."

In the nature of the soul is the compensation for the inequalities of condition. The radical tragedy of nature seems to be the distinction of More and Less. How can Less not feel the pain; how not feel indignation or malevolence towards More? Look at those who have less faculty, and one feels sad, and knows not well what to make of it. He almost shuns their eye; he fears they will upbraid God. What should they do? It seems a great injustice. But see the facts nearly, and these mountainous inequalities vanish. Love reduces them, as the sun melts the iceberg in the sea. The heart and soul of all men being one, this bitterness of *His* and *Mine* ceases. His is mine. I am my brother, and my brother is me. If I feel overshadowed and outdone by great neighbours, I can yet love; I can still receive; and he that loveth maketh his own the grandeur he loves. Thereby I make the discovery that my brother is my guardian, acting for me with the friendliest designs, and the estate I so admired and envied is my own. It is the nature of the soul to appropriate all things. Jesus and Shakespeare are fragments of the soul, and by love I conquer and incorporate them in my own conscious domain. His virtue,—is not that mine? His wit,—if it cannot be made mine, it is not wit.

Such, also, is the natural history of calamity. The changes which break up at short intervals the prosperity of men are advertisements of a nature whose law is growth. Every soul is by this intrinsic necessity quitting its whole system of things, its friends, and home, and laws, and faith, as the shell-fish crawls out of its beautiful but stony case, because it no longer admits of its growth, and slowly forms a new house. In proportion to the vigor of the individual, these revolutions are frequent, until in some happier mind they are incessant, and all worldly relations hang very loosely about him, becoming, as it were, a transparent fluid membrane through which the living form is seen, and not, as in most men, an indurated heterogeneous fabric of many dates, and of no settled character in which the man is imprisoned. Then there can be enlargement, and the man of to-day scarcely recognizes the man of yesterday. And such should be the outward biography of man in time, a putting off of dead circumstances day by day, as he renews his raiment day by day. But to us, in our lapsed estate, resting, not advancing, resisting, not cooperating with the divine expansion, this growth comes by shocks.

We cannot part with our friends. We cannot let our angels go. We do not see that they only go out, that archangels may come in. We are idolaters of the old. We do not believe in the riches of the soul, in its proper eternity and omnipresence. We do not believe there is any force in to-day to rival or recreate that beautiful yesterday. We linger in the ruins of the old tent, where once we had bread and shelter and organs, nor believe that the spirit can feed, cover, and nerve us again. We cannot again find aught so dear, so sweet, so graceful. But we sit and weep in vain. The voice of the Almighty saith, 'Up and onward for evermore!' We cannot stay amid the ruins. Neither will we rely on the new; and so we walk ever with reverted eyes, like those monsters who look backwards.

And yet the compensations of calamity are made apparent to the understanding also, after long intervals of time. A fever, a mutilation, a cruel disappointment, a loss of wealth, a loss of friends, seems at the moment unpaid loss, and unpayable. But the sure years reveal the deep remedial force that underlies all facts. The death of a dear friend, wife, brother, lover, which seemed nothing but privation, somewhat later assumes the aspect of a guide or genius; for it commonly operates revolutions in our way of life, terminates an epoch of infancy or of youth which was waiting to be closed, breaks up a wonted occupation, or a household, or style of living, and allows the formation of new ones more friendly to the growth of character. It permits or constrains the formation of new acquaintances, and the reception of new influences that prove of the first importance to the next years; and the man or woman who would have remained a sunny garden-flower, with no room for its roots and too much sunshine for its head, by the falling of the walls and the neglect of the gardener, is made the banian of the forest, yielding shade and fruit to wide neighbourhoods of men.

IV

THE OVER-SOUL

There is a difference between one and another hour of life, in their authority and subsequent effect. Our faith comes in moments; our vice is habitual. Yet there is a depth in those brief moments which constrains us to ascribe more reality to them than to all other experiences. For this reason, the argument which is always forthcoming to silence those who conceive extraordinary hopes of man, namely, the appeal to experience, is for ever invalid and vain. We give up the past to the objector, and yet we hope. He must explain this hope. We grant that human life is mean; but how did we find out that it was mean? What is the ground of this uneasiness of ours; of this old discontent? What is the universal sense of want and ignorance, but the fine innuendo by which the soul makes its enormous claim? Why do men feel that the natural history of man has never been written, but he is always leaving behind what you have said of him, and it becomes old, and books of metaphysics worthless? The philosophy of six thousand years has not searched the chambers and magazines of the soul. In its experiments there has always remained, in the last analysis, a residuum it could not resolve. Man is a stream whose source is hidden. Our being is descending into us from we know not whence. The most exact calculator has no prescience that somewhat incalculable may not balk the very next moment. I am constrained every moment to acknowledge a higher origin for events than the will I call mine.

As with events, so is it with thoughts. When I watch that flowing river, which, out of regions I see not, pours for a season its streams into me, I see that I am a pensioner; not a cause, but a surprised spectator of this ethereal water; that I desire and look up, and put myself in the attitude of reception, but from some alien energy the visions come.

The Supreme Critic on the errors of the past and the present, and the only prophet of that which must be, is that great nature in which we rest, as the earth lies in the soft arms of the atmosphere; that Unity, that Over-Soul, within which every man's particular being is contained and made one with all other; that common heart, of which all sincere conversation is the worship, to which all right action is submission; that overpowering reality which confutes our tricks and talents, and constrains every one to pass for what he is, and to speak from his character, and not from his tongue, and which evermore tends to pass into our thought and hand, and become wisdom, and virtue, and power, and beauty. We live in succession, in division, in parts, in particles. Meantime within man is the soul of the whole; the wise silence; the universal beauty, to which every part and particle is equally related; the eternal ONE. And this deep power in which we exist, and whose beatitude is all accessible to us, is not only self-sufficing and perfect in every hour, but the act of seeing and the thing seen, the seer and the spectacle, the subject and the object, are one. We see the world piece by piece, as the sun, the moon, the animal, the tree; but the whole, of which these are the shining parts, is the soul. Only by the vision of that Wisdom can the horoscope of the ages be read, and by falling back on our better thoughts, by yielding to the spirit of prophecy which is innate in every man, we can know what it saith. Every man's words, who speaks from that life, must sound vain to those who do not dwell in the same thought on their own part. I dare not speak for it. My words do not carry its august sense; they fall short and cold. Only itself can inspire whom it will, and behold! their speech shall be lyrical, and sweet, and universal as the rising of the wind. Yet I desire, even by profane words, if I may not use sacred, to indicate the heaven of this deity, and to report what hints I have collected of the transcendent simplicity and energy of the Highest Law.

If we consider what happens in conversation, in reveries, in remorse, in times of passion, in surprises, in the instructions of dreams, wherein often we see ourselves in masquerade,—the droll disguises only magnifying and enhancing a real element, and forcing it on our distinct notice,—we shall catch many hints that will broaden and lighten into knowledge of the secret of nature. All goes to show that the soul in man is not an organ, but animates and exercises all the organs; is not a function, like the power of memory, of calculation, of comparison, but uses these as hands and feet; is not a faculty, but a light; is not the intellect or the will, but the master of the intellect and the will; is the background of our being, in which they lie,—an immensity not possessed and that cannot be possessed. From within or from behind, a light shines through us upon things, and makes us aware that we are nothing, but the light is all. A man is the facade of a temple wherein all wisdom and all good abide. What we commonly call man, the eating, drinking, planting, counting man, does not, as we know him, represent himself, but misrepresents himself. Him we do not respect, but the soul, whose organ he is, would he let it appear through his action, would make our knees bend. When it breathes through his intellect, it is genius; when it breathes through his will, it is virtue; when it flows through his affection, it is love. And the blindness of the intellect begins, when it would be something of itself. The weakness of the will begins, when the individual would be something of himself. All reform aims, in some one particular, to let the soul have its way through us; in other words, to engage us to obey.

Of this pure nature every man is at some time sensible. Language cannot paint it with his colors. It is too subtle. It is indefinable, unmeasurable, but we know that it pervades and contains us. We know that all spiritual being is in man. A wise old proverb says, "God comes to see us without bell"; that is, as there is no screen or ceiling between our heads and the infinite heavens, so is there no bar or wall in the soul where man, the effect, ceases, and God, the cause, begins. The walls are taken away. We lie open on one side to the deeps of spiritual nature, to the attributes of God. Justice we see and know, Love, Freedom, Power. These natures no man ever got above, but they tower over us, and most in the moment when our interests tempt us to wound them.

The sovereignty of this nature whereof we speak is made known by its independency of those limitations which circumscribe us on every hand. The soul circumscribes all things. As I have said, it contradicts all experience. In like manner it abolishes time and space. The influence of the senses has, in most men, overpowered the mind to that degree, that the walls of time and space have come to look real and insurmountable; and to speak with levity of these limits is, in the world, the sign of insanity. Yet time and space are but inverse measures of the force of the soul. The spirit sports with time,—

"Can crowd eternity into an hour,
   Or stretch an hour to eternity."

We are often made to feel that there is another youth and age than that which is measured from the year of our natural birth. Some thoughts always find us young, and keep us so. Such a thought is the love of the universal and eternal beauty. Every man parts from that contemplation with the feeling that it rather belongs to ages than to mortal life. The least activity of the intellectual powers redeems us in a degree from the conditions of time. In sickness, in languor, give us a strain of poetry, or a profound sentence, and we are refreshed; or produce a volume of Plato, or Shakespeare, or remind us of their names, and instantly we come into a feeling of longevity. See how the deep, divine thought reduces centuries, and millenniums, and makes itself present through all ages. Is the teaching of Christ less effective now than it was when first his mouth was opened? The emphasis of facts and persons in my thought has nothing to do with time. And so, always, the soul's scale is one; the scale of the senses and the understanding is another. Before the revelations of the soul, Time, Space, and Nature shrink away. In common speech, we refer all things to time, as we habitually refer the immensely sundered stars to one concave sphere. And so we say that the Judgment is distant or near, that the Millennium approaches, that a day of certain political, moral, social reforms is at hand, and the like, when we mean, that, in the nature of things, one of the facts we contemplate is external and fugitive, and the other is permanent and connate with the soul. The things we now esteem fixed shall, one by one, detach themselves, like ripe fruit, from our experience, and fall. The wind shall blow them none knows whither. The landscape, the figures, Boston, London, are facts as fugitive as any institution past, or any whiff of mist or smoke, and so is society, and so is the world. The soul looketh steadily forwards, creating a world before her, leaving worlds behind her. She has no dates, nor rites, nor persons, nor specialties, nor men. The soul knows only the soul; the web of events is the flowing robe in which she is clothed.

After its own law and not by arithmetic is the rate of its progress to be computed. The soul's advances are not made by gradation, such as can be represented by motion in a straight line; but rather by ascension of state, such as can be represented by metamorphosis,— from the egg to the worm, from the worm to the fly. The growths of genius are of a certain total character, that does not advance the elect individual first over John, then Adam, then Richard, and give to each the pain of discovered inferiority, but by every throe of growth the man expands there where he works, passing, at each pulsation, classes, populations, of men. With each divine impulse the mind rends the thin rinds of the visible and finite, and comes out into eternity, and inspires and expires its air. It converses with truths that have always been spoken in the world, and becomes conscious of a closer sympathy with Zeno and Arrian, than with persons in the house.

This is the law of moral and of mental gain. The simple rise as by specific levity, not into a particular virtue, but into the region of all the virtues. They are in the spirit which contains them all. The soul requires purity, but purity is not it; requires justice, but justice is not that; requires beneficence, but is somewhat better; so that there is a kind of descent and accommodation felt when we leave speaking of moral nature, to urge a virtue which it enjoins. To the well-born child, all the virtues are natural, and not painfully acquired. Speak to his heart, and the man becomes suddenly virtuous.

Within the same sentiment is the germ of intellectual growth, which obeys the same law. Those who are capable of humility, of justice, of love, of aspiration, stand already on a platform that commands the sciences and arts, speech and poetry, action and grace. For whoso dwells in this moral beatitude already anticipates those special powers which men prize so highly. The lover has no talent, no skill, which passes for quite nothing with his enamoured maiden, however little she may possess of related faculty; and the heart which abandons itself to the Supreme Mind finds itself related to all its works, and will travel a royal road to particular knowledges and powers. In ascending to this primary and aboriginal sentiment, we have come from our remote station on the circumference instantaneously to the centre of the world, where, as in the closet of God, we see causes, and anticipate the universe, which is but a slow effect.

One mode of the divine teaching is the incarnation of the spirit in a form,—in forms, like my own. I live in society; with persons who answer to thoughts in my own mind, or express a certain obedience to the great instincts to which I live. I see its presence to them. I am certified of a common nature; and these other souls, these separated selves, draw me as nothing else can. They stir in me the new emotions we call passion; of love, hatred, fear, admiration, pity; thence comes conversation, competition, persuasion, cities, and war. Persons are supplementary to the primary teaching of the soul. In youth we are mad for persons. Childhood and youth see all the world in them. But the larger experience of man discovers the identical nature appearing through them all. Persons themselves acquaint us with the impersonal. In all conversation between two persons, tacit reference is made, as to a third party, to a common nature. That third party or common nature is not social; it is impersonal; is God. And so in groups where debate is earnest, and especially on high questions, the company become aware that the thought rises to an equal level in all bosoms, that all have a spiritual property in what was said, as well as the sayer. They all become wiser than they were. It arches over them like a temple, this unity of thought, in which every heart beats with nobler sense of power and duty, and thinks and acts with unusual solemnity. All are conscious of attaining to a higher self-possession. It shines for all. There is a certain wisdom of humanity which is common to the greatest men with the lowest, and which our ordinary education often labors to silence and obstruct. The mind is one, and the best minds, who love truth for its own sake, think much less of property in truth. They accept it thankfully everywhere, and do not label or stamp it with any man's name, for it is theirs long beforehand, and from eternity. The learned and the studious of thought have no monopoly of wisdom. Their violence of direction in some degree disqualifies them to think truly. We owe many valuable observations to people who are not very acute or profound, and who say the thing without effort, which we want and have long been hunting in vain. The action of the soul is oftener in that which is felt and left unsaid, than in that which is said in any conversation. It broods over every society, and they unconsciously seek for it in each other. We know better than we do. We do not yet possess ourselves, and we know at the same time that we are much more. I feel the same truth how often in my trivial conversation with my neighbours, that somewhat higher in each of us overlooks this by-play, and Jove nods to Jove from behind each of us.

Men descend to meet. In their habitual and mean service to the world, for which they forsake their native nobleness, they resemble those Arabian sheiks, who dwell in mean houses, and affect an external poverty, to escape the rapacity of the Pacha, and reserve all their display of wealth for their interior and guarded retirements.

As it is present in all persons, so it is in every period of life. It is adult already in the infant man. In my dealing with my child, my Latin and Greek, my accomplishments and my money stead me nothing; but as much soul as I have avails. If I am wilful, he sets his will against mine, one for one, and leaves me, if I please, the degradation of beating him by my superiority of strength. But if I renounce my will, and act for the soul, setting that up as umpire between us two, out of his young eyes looks the same soul; he reveres and loves with me.

The soul is the perceiver and revealer of truth. We know truth when we see it, let skeptic and scoffer say what they choose. Foolish people ask you, when you have spoken what they do not wish to hear, 'How do you know it is truth, and not an error of your own?' We know truth when we see it, from opinion, as we know when we are awake that we are awake. It was a grand sentence of Emanuel Swedenborg, which would alone indicate the greatness of that man's perception,—"It is no proof of a man's understanding to be able to confirm whatever he pleases; but to be able to discern that what is true is true, and that what is false is false, this is the mark and character of intelligence." In the book I read, the good thought returns to me, as every truth will, the image of the whole soul. To the bad thought which I find in it, the same soul becomes a discerning, separating sword, and lops it away. We are wiser than we know. If we will not interfere with our thought, but will act entirely, or see how the thing stands in God, we know the particular thing, and every thing, and every man. For the Maker of all things and all persons stands behind us, and casts his dread omniscience through us over things.

But beyond this recognition of its own in particular passages of the individual's experience, it also reveals truth. And here we should seek to reinforce ourselves by its very presence, and to speak with a worthier, loftier strain of that advent. For the soul's communication of truth is the highest event in nature, since it then does not give somewhat from itself, but it gives itself, or passes into and becomes that man whom it enlightens; or, in proportion to that truth he receives, it takes him to itself.

We distinguish the announcements of the soul, its manifestations of its own nature, by the term *Revelation*. These are always attended by the emotion of the sublime. For this communication is an influx of the Divine mind into our mind. It is an ebb of the individual rivulet before the flowing surges of the sea of life. Every distinct apprehension of this central commandment agitates men with awe and delight. A thrill passes through all men at the reception of new truth, or at the performance of a great action, which comes out of the heart of nature. In these communications, the power to see is not separated from the will to do, but the insight proceeds from obedience, and the obedience proceeds from a joyful perception. Every moment when the individual feels himself invaded by it is

memorable. By the necessity of our constitution, a certain enthusiasm attends the individual's consciousness of that divine presence.
The character and duration of this enthusiasm varies with the state
of the individual, from an ecstasy and trance and prophetic inspiration,—which is its rarer appearance,—to the faintest glow of
virtuous emotion, in which form it warms, like our household fires,
all the families and associations of men, and makes society possible.
A certain tendency to insanity has always attended the opening of
the religious sense in men, as if they had been "blasted with excess
of light." The trances of Socrates, the "union" of Plotinus, the vision
of Porphyry, the conversion of Paul, the aurora of Behmen, the
convulsions of George Fox and his Quakers, the illumination of
Swedenborg, are of this kind. What was in the case of these remarkable persons a ravishment has, in innumerable instances in common
life, been exhibited in less striking manner. Everywhere the history
of religion betrays a tendency to enthusiasm. The rapture of the
Moravian and Quietist; the opening of the internal sense of the Word,
in the language of the New Jerusalem Church; the *revival* of the
Calvinistic churches; the *experiences* of the Methodists, are varying
forms of that shudder of awe and delight with which the individual
soul always mingles with the universal soul.

The nature of these revelations is the same; they are perceptions
of the absolute law. They are solutions of the soul's own questions.
They do not answer the questions which the understanding asks.
The soul answers never by words, but by the thing itself that is
inquired after.

Revelation is the disclosure of the soul. The popular notion of a
revelation is, that it is a telling of fortunes. In past oracles of the soul,
the understanding seeks to find answers to sensual questions, and
undertakes to tell from God how long men shall exist, what their
hands shall do, and who shall be their company, adding names, and
dates, and places. But we must pick no locks. We must check this low

curiosity. An answer in words is delusive; it is really no answer to the questions you ask. Do not require a description of the countries towards which you sail. The description does not describe them to you, and to-morrow you arrive there, and know them by inhabiting them. Men ask concerning the immortality of the soul, the employments of heaven, the state of the sinner, and so forth. They even dream that Jesus has left replies to precisely these interrogatories. Never a moment did that sublime spirit speak in their *patois*. To truth, justice, love, the attributes of the soul, the idea of immutableness is essentially associated. Jesus, living in these moral sentiments, heedless of sensual fortunes, heeding only the manifestations of these, never made the separation of the idea of duration from the essence of these attributes, nor uttered a syllable concerning the duration of the soul. It was left to his disciples to sever duration from the moral elements, and to teach the immortality of the soul as a doctrine, and maintain it by evidences. The moment the doctrine of the immortality is separately taught, man is already fallen. In the flowing of love, in the adoration of humility, there is no question of continuance. No inspired man ever asks this question, or condescends to these evidences. For the soul is true to itself, and the man in whom it is shed abroad cannot wander from the present, which is infinite, to a future which would be finite.

These questions which we lust to ask about the future are a confession of sin. God has no answer for them. No answer in words can reply to a question of things. It is not in an arbitrary "decree of God," but in the nature of man, that a veil shuts down on the facts of to-morrow; for the soul will not have us read any other cipher than that of cause and effect. By this veil, which curtains events, it instructs the children of men to live in to-day. The only mode of obtaining an answer to these questions of the senses is to forego all low curiosity, and, accepting the tide of being which floats us into the secret of nature, work and live, work and live, and all unawares the advancing soul has built and forged for itself a new condition, and the question and the answer are one.

By the same fire, vital, consecrating, celestial, which burns until it shall dissolve all things into the waves and surges of an ocean of light, we see and know each other, and what spirit each is of. Who can tell the grounds of his knowledge of the character of the several individuals in his circle of friends? No man. Yet their acts and words do not disappoint him. In that man, though he knew no ill of him, he put no trust. In that other, though they had seldom met, authentic signs had yet passed, to signify that he might be trusted as one who had an interest in his own character. We know each other very well,—which of us has been just to himself, and whether that which we teach or behold is only an aspiration, or is our honest effort also.

We are all discerners of spirits. That diagnosis lies aloft in our life or unconscious power. The intercourse of society,—its trade, its religion, its friendships, its quarrels,—is one wide, judicial investigation of character. In full court, or in small committee, or confronted face to face, accuser and accused, men offer themselves to be judged. Against their will they exhibit those decisive trifles by which character is read. But who judges? and what? Not our understanding. We do not read them by learning or craft. No; the wisdom of the wise man consists herein, that he does not judge them; he lets them judge themselves, and merely reads and records their own verdict.

By virtue of this inevitable nature, private will is overpowered, and, maugre our efforts or our imperfections, your genius will speak from you, and mine from me. That which we are, we shall teach, not voluntarily, but involuntarily. Thoughts come into our minds by avenues which we never left open, and thoughts go out of our minds through avenues which we never voluntarily opened. Character teaches over our head. The infallible index of true progress is found in the tone the man takes. Neither his age, nor his breeding, nor company, nor books, nor actions, nor talents, nor all together, can hinder him from being deferential to a higher spirit than his own. If he have not found his home in God, his manners, his forms of speech, the turn of his sentences, the build, shall I say, of all his opinions, will involuntarily confess it, let him brave it out how he will. If he have found his centre, the Deity will shine through him, through all the disguises of ignorance, of ungenial temperament, of unfavorable circumstance. The tone of seeking is one, and the tone of having is another.

The great distinction between teachers sacred or literary,— between poets like Herbert, and poets like Pope,—between philosophers like Spinoza, Kant, and Coleridge, and philosophers like Locke, Paley, Mackintosh, and Stewart,—between men of the world, who are reckoned accomplished talkers, and here and there a fervent mystic, prophesying, half insane under the infinitude of his thought,—is, that one class speak *from within*, or from experience, as parties and possessors of the fact; and the other class, *from without*, as spectators merely, or perhaps as acquainted with the fact on the evidence of third persons. It is of no use to preach to me from without. I can do that too easily myself. Jesus speaks always from within, and in a degree that transcends all others. In that is the miracle. I believe beforehand that it ought so to be. All men stand continually in the expectation of the appearance of such a teacher. But if a man do not speak from within the veil, where the word is one with that it tells of, let him lowly confess it.

The same Omniscience flows into the intellect, and makes what we call genius. Much of the wisdom of the world is not wisdom, and the most illuminated class of men are no doubt superior to literary fame, and are not writers. Among the multitude of scholars and authors, we feel no hallowing presence; we are sensible of a knack and skill rather than of inspiration; they have a light, and know not whence it comes, and call it their own; their talent is some exaggerated faculty, some overgrown member, so that their strength is a disease. In these instances the intellectual gifts do not make the impression of virtue, but almost of vice; and we feel that a man's talents stand in the way of his advancement in truth. But genius is religious. It is a larger imbibing of the common heart. It is not anomalous, but more like, and not less like other men. There is, in all great poets, a wisdom of humanity which is superior to any talents they exercise. The author, the wit, the partisan, the fine gentleman, does not take place of the man. Humanity shines in Homer, in Chaucer, in Spenser, in Shakespeare, in Milton. They are content with truth. They use the positive degree. They seem frigid and phlegmatic to those who have been spiced with the frantic passion and violent coloring of inferior, but popular writers. For they are poets by the free course which they allow to the informing soul, which through their eyes beholds again, and blesses the things which it hath made. The soul is superior to its knowledge; wiser than any of its works. The great poet makes us feel our own wealth, and then we think less of his compositions. His best communication to our mind is to teach us to despise all he has done. Shakespeare carries us to such a lofty strain of intelligent activity, as to suggest a wealth which beggars his own; and we then feel that the splendid works which he has created, and which in other hours we extol as a sort of self-existent poetry, take no stronger hold of real nature than the shadow of a passing traveller on the rock. The inspiration which uttered itself in Hamlet and Lear could utter things as good from day to day, for ever. Why, then, should I make account of Hamlet and Lear, as if we had not the soul from which they fell as syllables from the tongue?

This energy does not descend into individual life on any other condition than entire possession. It comes to the lowly and simple; it comes to whomsoever will put off what is foreign and proud; it comes as insight; it comes as serenity and grandeur. When we see those whom it inhabits, we are apprized of new degrees of greatness. From that inspiration the man comes back with a changed tone. He does not talk with men with an eye to their opinion. He tries them. It requires of us to be plain and true. The vain traveller attempts to embellish his life by quoting my lord, and the prince, and the countess, who thus said or did to him. The ambitious vulgar show you their spoons, and brooches, and rings, and preserve their cards and compliments. The more cultivated, in their account of their own experience, cull out the pleasing, poetic circumstance,—the visit to Rome, the man of genius they saw, the brilliant friend they know; still further on, perhaps, the gorgeous landscape, the mountain lights, the mountain thoughts, they enjoyed yesterday,—and so seek to throw a romantic color over their life. But the soul that ascends to worship the great God is plain and true; has no rose-color, no fine friends, no chivalry, no adventures; does not want admiration; dwells in the hour that now is, in the earnest experience of the common day,—by reason of the present moment and the mere trifle having become porous to thought, and bibulous of the sea of light.

Converse with a mind that is grandly simple, and literature looks like word-catching. The simplest utterances are worthiest to be written, yet are they so cheap, and so things of course, that, in the infinite riches of the soul, it is like gathering a few pebbles off the ground, or bottling a little air in a phial, when the whole earth and the whole atmosphere are ours. Nothing can pass there, or make you one of the circle, but the casting aside your trappings, and dealing man to man in naked truth, plain confession, and omniscient affirmation.

Souls such as these treat you as gods would; walk as gods in the earth, accepting without any admiration your wit, your bounty, your virtue even,—say rather your act of duty, for your virtue they own as their proper blood, royal as themselves, and over-royal, and the father of the gods. But what rebuke their plain fraternal bearing casts on the mutual flattery with which authors solace each other and wound themselves! These flatter not. I do not wonder that these men go to see Cromwell, and Christina, and Charles the Second, and James the

First, and the Grand Turk. For they are, in their own elevation, the fellows of kings, and must feel the servile tone of conversation in the world. They must always be a godsend to princes, for they confront them, a king to a king, without ducking or concession, and give a high nature the refreshment and satisfaction of resistance, of plain humanity, of even companionship, and of new ideas. They leave them wiser and superior men. Souls like these make us feel that sincerity is more excellent than flattery. Deal so plainly with man and woman, as to constrain the utmost sincerity, and destroy all hope of trifling with you. It is the highest compliment you can pay. Their "highest praising," said Milton, "is not flattery, and their plainest advice is a kind of praising."

Ineffable is the union of man and God in every act of the soul. The simplest person, who in his integrity worships God, becomes God; yet for ever and ever the influx of this better and universal self is new and unsearchable. It inspires awe and astonishment. How dear, how soothing to man, arises the idea of God, peopling the lonely place, effacing the scars of our mistakes and disappointments! When we have broken our god of tradition, and ceased from our god of rhetoric, then may God fire the heart with his presence. It is the doubling of the heart itself, nay, the infinite enlargement of the heart with a power of growth to a new infinity on every side. It inspires in man an infallible trust. He has not the conviction, but the sight, that the best is the true, and may in that thought easily dismiss all particular uncertainties and fears, and adjourn to the sure revelation of time, the solution of his private riddles. He is sure that his welfare is dear to the heart of being. In the presence of law to his mind, he is overflowed with a reliance so universal, that it sweeps away all cherished hopes and the most stable projects of mortal condition in its flood. He believes that he cannot escape from his good. The things that are really for thee gravitate to thee. You are running to seek your friend. Let your feet run, but your mind need not. If you do not find him, will you not acquiesce that it is best you should not find him? for there is a power, which, as it is in you, is in him also, and could therefore very well bring you together, if it were for the best. You are preparing with eagerness to go and render a service to which your talent and your taste invite you, the love of men and the hope of fame. Has it not occurred to you, that you have no right to go, unless you are equally willing to be prevented from going? O, believe, as thou livest, that every sound that is spoken over the round world, which thou oughtest to hear, will vibrate on thine ear! Every proverb, every book, every byword that belongs to thee for aid or comfort, shall surely come home through open or winding passages. Every friend whom not thy fantastic will, but the great and tender heart in thee craveth, shall lock thee in his embrace. And this, because the heart in thee is the heart of all; not a valve, not a wall, not an intersection is there anywhere in nature, but one blood rolls uninterruptedly an endless circulation through all men, as the water of the globe is all one sea, and, truly seen, its tide is one.

Let man, then, learn the revelation of all nature and all thought to his heart; this, namely; that the Highest dwells with him; that the sources of nature are in his own mind, if the sentiment of duty is there. But if he would know what the great God speaketh, he must 'go into his closet and shut the door,' as Jesus said. God will not make himself manifest to cowards. He must greatly listen to himself, withdrawing himself from all the accents of other men's devotion. Even their prayers are hurtful to him, until he have made his own. Our religion vulgarly stands on numbers of believers. Whenever the appeal is made—no matter how indirectly—to numbers, proclamation is then and there made, that religion is not. He that finds God a sweet, enveloping thought to him never counts his company. When I sit in that presence, who shall dare to come in? When I rest in perfect humility, when I burn with pure love, what can Calvin or Swedenborg say?

It makes no difference whether the appeal is to numbers or to one. The faith that stands on authority is not faith. The reliance on authority measures the decline of religion, the withdrawal of the soul. The position men have given to Jesus, now for many centuries of history, is a position of authority. It characterizes themselves. It cannot alter the eternal facts. Great is the soul, and plain. It is no flatterer, it is no follower; it never appeals from itself. It believes in itself. Before the immense possibilities of man, all mere experience, all past biography, however spotless and sainted, shrinks away. Before that heaven which our presentiments foreshow us, we cannot easily praise any form of life we have seen or read of. We not only affirm that we have few great men, but, absolutely speaking, that we have none; that we have no history, no record of any character or mode of living, that entirely contents us. The saints and demigods whom history worships we are constrained to accept with a grain of allowance. Though in our lonely hours we draw a new strength out of their memory, yet, pressed on our attention, as they are by the thoughtless and customary, they fatigue and invade. The soul gives itself, alone, original, and pure, to the Lonely, Original, and Pure, who, on that condition, gladly inhabits, leads, and speaks through it. Then is it glad, young, and nimble. It is not wise, but it sees through all things. It is not called religious, but it is innocent. It calls the light its own, and feels that the grass grows and the stone falls by a law inferior to, and dependent on, its nature. Behold, it saith, I am born into the great, the universal mind. I, the imperfect, adore my own Perfect. I am somehow receptive of the great soul, and thereby I do overlook the sun and the stars, and feel them to be the fair accidents and effects which change and pass. More and more the surges of everlasting nature enter into me, and I become public and human in my regards and actions. So come I to live in thoughts, and act with energies, which are immortal. Thus revering the soul, and learning, as the ancient said, that "its beauty is immense," man will come to see that the world is the perennial miracle which the soul worketh, and be less astonished at particular wonders; he will learn that there is no profane history; that all history is sacred; that the universe is represented in an atom, in a moment of time. He will weave no longer a spotted life of shreds and patches, but he will live with a divine unity. He will cease from what is base and frivolous in his life, and be content with all places and with any service he can render. He will calmly front the morrow in the negligency of that trust which carries God with it, and so hath already the whole future in the bottom of the heart.

V

SELF-RELIANCE

I read the other day some verses written by an eminent painter which were original and not conventional. The soul always hears an admonition in such lines, let the subject be what it may. The sentiment they instill is of more value than any thought they may contain. To believe your own thought, to believe that what is true for you in your private heart is true for all men,—that is genius. Speak your latent conviction, and it shall be the universal sense; for the inmost in due time becomes the outmost,—and our first thought is rendered back to us by the trumpets of the Last Judgment. Familiar as the voice of the mind is to each, the highest merit we ascribe to Moses, Plato, and Milton is, that they set at naught books and traditions, and spoke not what men but what they thought. A man should learn to detect and watch that gleam of light which flashes across his mind from within, more than the luster of the firmament of bards and sages. Yet he dismisses without notice his thought, because it is his. In every work of genius we recognize our own rejected thoughts: they come back to us with a certain alienated majesty. Great works of art have no more affecting lesson for us than this. They teach us to abide by our spontaneous impression with good-humored inflexibility then most when the whole cry of voices is on the other side. Else, to-morrow a stranger will say with masterly good sense precisely what we have thought and felt all the time, and we shall be forced to take with shame our own opinion from another.

There is a time in every man's education when he arrives at the conviction that envy is ignorance; that imitation is suicide; that he must take himself for better, for worse, as his portion; that though the wide universe is full of good, no kernel of nourishing corn can come to him but through his toil bestowed on that plot of ground which is given to him to till. The power which resides in him is new in nature, and none but he knows what that is which he can do, nor does he know until he has tried. Not for nothing one face, one character, one fact, makes much impression on him, and another none. This sculpture in the memory is not without pre-established harmony. The eye was placed where one ray should fall, that it might testify of that particular ray. We but half express ourselves, and are ashamed of that divine idea which each of us represents. It may be safely trusted as proportionate and of good issues, so it be faithfully imparted, but God will not have his work made manifest by cowards. A man is relieved and gay when he has put his heart into his work and done his best; but what he has said or done otherwise, shall give him no peace. It is a deliverance which does not deliver. In the attempt his genius deserts him; no muse befriends; no invention, no hope.

Trust thyself: every heart vibrates to that iron string. Accept the place the divine providence has found for you, the society of your contemporaries, the connection of events. Great men have always done so, and confided themselves childlike to the genius of their age, betraying their perception that the absolutely trustworthy was seated at their heart, working through their hands, predominating in all their being. And we are now men, and must accept in the highest mind the same transcendent destiny; and not minors and invalids in a protected corner, not cowards fleeing before a revolution, but guides, redeemers, and benefactors, obeying the Almighty effort, and advancing on Chaos and the Dark.

What pretty oracles nature yields us on this text, in the face and behaviour of children, babes, and even brutes! That divided and rebel mind, that distrust of a sentiment because our arithmetic has computed the strength and means opposed to our purpose, these have not. Their mind being whole, their eye is as yet unconquered, and when we look in their faces, we are disconcerted. Infancy conforms to nobody: all conform to it, so that one babe commonly makes four or five out of the adults who prattle and play to it. So God has armed youth and puberty and manhood no less with its own piquancy and charm, and made it enviable and gracious and its claims not to be put by, if it will stand by itself. Do not think the youth has no force, because he cannot speak to you and me. Hark! in the next room his voice is sufficiently clear and emphatic. It seems he knows how to speak to his contemporaries. Bashful or bold, then, he will know how to make us seniors very unnecessary.

The nonchalance of boys who are sure of a dinner, and would disdain as much as a lord to do or say aught to conciliate one, is the healthy attitude of human nature. A boy is in the parlour what the pit is in the playhouse; independent, irresponsible, looking out from his corner on such people and facts as pass by, he tries and sentences them on their merits, in the swift, summary way of boys, as good, bad, interesting, silly, eloquent, troublesome. He cumbers himself never about consequences, about interests: he gives an independent, genuine verdict. You must court him: he does not court you. But the man is, as it were, clapped into jail by his consciousness. As soon as he has once acted or spoken with eclat, he is a committed person, watched by the sympathy or the hatred of hundreds, whose affections must now enter into his account. There is no Lethe for this. Ah, that he could pass again into his neutrality! Who can thus avoid all pledges, and having observed, observe again from the same unaffected, unbiased, unbribable, unaffrighted innocence, must always be formidable. He would utter opinions on all passing affairs, which being seen to be not private, but necessary, would sink like darts into the ear of men, and put them in fear.

These are the voices which we hear in solitude, but they grow faint and inaudible as we enter into the world. Society everywhere is in conspiracy against the manhood of every one of its members. Society is a joint-stock company, in which the members agree, for the better securing of his bread to each shareholder, to surrender the liberty and culture of the eater. The virtue in most request is conformity. Self-reliance is its aversion. It loves not realities and creators, but names and customs.

Whoso would be a man must be a nonconformist. He who would gather immortal palms must not be hindered by the name of goodness, but must explore if it be goodness. Nothing is at last sacred but the integrity of your own mind. Absolve you to yourself, and you shall have the suffrage of the world. I remember an answer which when quite young I was prompted to make to a valued adviser, who was wont to importune me with the dear old doctrines of the church. On my saying, What have I to do with the sacredness of traditions, if I live wholly from within? my friend suggested,—"But these impulses may be from below, not from above." I replied, "They do not seem to me to be such; but if I am the Devil's child, I will live then from the Devil." No law can be sacred to me but that of my nature. Good and bad are but names very readily transferable to that or this; the only right is what is after my constitution, the only wrong what is against it. A man is to carry himself in the presence of all opposition, as if every thing were titular and ephemeral but he. I am ashamed to think how easily we capitulate to badges and names, to large societies and dead institutions. Every decent and well-spoken individual affects and sways me more than is right. I ought to go upright and vital, and speak the rude truth in all ways. If malice and vanity wear the coat of philanthropy, shall that pass? If an angry bigot assumes this bountiful cause of Abolition, and comes to me with his last news from Barbadoes, why should I not say to him, 'Go love thy infant; love thy wood-chopper: be good-natured and modest: have that grace; and never varnish your hard, uncharitable ambition with this incredible tenderness for black folk a thousand miles off. Thy love afar is spite at home.' Rough and graceless would be such greeting, but truth is handsomer than the affectation of love. Your goodness must have some edge to it,—else it is none. The doctrine of hatred must be preached as the counteraction of the doctrine of love when that pules and whines. I shun father and mother and wife and brother, when my genius calls me. I would write on the lintels of the door-post, Whim. I hope it is somewhat better than whim at last, but we cannot spend the day in explanation. Expect me not to show cause why I seek or why I exclude company. Then, again, do not tell me, as a good man did to-day, of my obligation to put all poor men in good situations. Are they my poor? I tell thee, thou foolish philanthropist, that I grudge the dollar, the dime, the cent, I give to such men as do not belong to me and to whom I do not belong. There is a class of persons to whom by all spiritual affinity I am bought and sold; for them I will go to prison, if need be; but your miscellaneous popular charities; the education at college of fools; the building of meeting-houses to the vain end to which many now stand; alms to sots; and the thousandfold Relief Societies;—though I confess with shame I sometimes succumb and give the dollar, it is a wicked dollar which by and by I shall have the manhood to withhold.

Virtues are, in the popular estimate, rather the exception than the rule. There is the man and his virtues. Men do what is called a good action, as some piece of courage or charity, much as they would pay a fine in expiation of daily non-appearance on parade. Their works are done as an apology or extenuation of their living in the world,—as invalids and the insane pay a high board. Their virtues are penances. I do not wish to expiate, but to live. My life is for itself and not for a spectacle. I much prefer that it should be of a lower strain, so it be genuine and equal, than that it should be glittering and unsteady. I wish it to be sound and sweet, and not to need diet and bleeding. I ask primary evidence that you are a man, and refuse this appeal from the man to his actions. I know that for myself it makes no difference whether I do or forbear those actions which are reckoned excellent. I cannot consent to pay for a privilege where I have intrinsic right. Few and mean as my gifts may be, I actually am, and do not need for my own assurance or the assurance of my fellows any secondary testimony.

What I must do is all that concerns me, not what the people think. This rule, equally arduous in actual and in intellectual life, may serve for the whole distinction between greatness and meanness. It is the harder, because you will always find those who think they know what is your duty better than you know it. It is easy in the world to live after the world's opinion; it is easy in solitude to live after our own; but the great man is he who in the midst of the crowd keeps with perfect sweetness the independence of solitude.

The objection to conforming to usages that have become dead to you is, that it scatters your force. It loses your time and blurs the impression of your character. If you maintain a dead church, contribute to a dead Bible-society, vote with a great party either for the government or against it, spread your table like base housekeepers,— under all these screens I have difficulty to detect the precise man you are. And, of course, so much force is withdrawn from your proper life. But do your work, and I shall know you. Do your work, and you shall reinforce yourself. A man must consider what a blindman's-buff is this game of conformity. If I know your sect, I anticipate your argument. I hear a preacher announce for his text and topic the expediency of one of the institutions of his church. Do I not know beforehand that not possibly can he say a new and spontaneous word?

Do I not know that, with all this ostentation of examining the grounds of the institution, he will do no such thing? Do I not know that he is pledged to himself not to look but at one side,—the permitted side, not as a man, but as a parish minister? He is a retained attorney, and these airs of the bench are the emptiest affectation. Well, most men have bound their eyes with one or another handkerchief, and attached themselves to some one of these communities of opinion. This conformity makes them not false in a few particulars, authors of a few lies, but false in all particulars. Their every truth is not quite true. Their two is not the real two, their four not the real four; so that every word they say chagrins us, and we know not where to begin to set them right. Meantime nature is not slow to equip us in the prison-uniform of the party to which we adhere. We come to wear one cut of face and figure, and acquire by degrees the gentlest asinine expression. There is a mortifying experience in particular, which does not fail to wreak itself also in the general history; I mean "the foolish face of praise," the forced smile which we put on in company where we do not feel at ease in answer to conversation which does not interest us. The muscles, not spontaneously moved, but moved by a low usurping wilfulness, grow tight about the outline of the face with the most disagreeable sensation.

For nonconformity the world whips you with its displeasure. And therefore a man must know how to estimate a sour face. The by-standers look askance on him in the public street or in the friend's parlour. If this aversation had its origin in contempt and resistance like his own, he might well go home with a sad countenance; but the sour faces of the multitude, like their sweet faces, have no deep cause, but are put on and off as the wind blows and a newspaper directs. Yet is the discontent of the multitude more formidable than that of the senate and the college. It is easy enough for a firm man who knows the world to brook the rage of the cultivated classes. Their rage is decorous and prudent, for they are timid as being very vulnerable themselves. But when to their feminine rage the indignation of the people is added, when the ignorant and the poor are aroused, when the unintelligent brute force that lies at the bottom of society is made to growl and mow, it needs the habit of magnanimity and religion to treat it godlike as a trifle of no concernment.

The other terror that scares us from self-trust is our consistency; a reverence for our past act or word, because the eyes of others have no other data for computing our orbit than our past acts, and we are loath to disappoint them.

But why should you keep your head over your shoulder? Why drag about this corpse of your memory, lest you contradict somewhat you have stated in this or that public place? Suppose you should contradict yourself; what then? It seems to be a rule of wisdom never to rely on your memory alone, scarcely even in acts of pure memory, but to bring the past for judgment into the thousand-eyed present, and live ever in a new day. In your metaphysics you have denied personality to the Deity: yet when the devout motions of the soul come, yield to them heart and life, though they should clothe God with shape and color. Leave your theory, as Joseph his coat in the hand of the harlot, and flee.

A foolish consistency is the hobgoblin of little minds, adored by little statesmen and philosophers and divines. With consistency a great soul has simply nothing to do. He may as well concern himself with his shadow on the wall. Speak what you think now in hard words, and to-morrow speak what to-morrow thinks in hard words again, though it contradict every thing you said to-day.—'Ah, so you shall be sure to be misunderstood.'—Is it so bad, then, to be misunderstood? Pythagoras was misunderstood, and Socrates, and Jesus, and Luther, and Copernicus, and Galileo, and Newton, and every pure and wise spirit that ever took flesh. To be great is to be misunderstood.

I suppose no man can violate his nature. All the sallies of his will are rounded in by the law of his being, as the inequalities of Andes and Himmaleh are insignificant in the curve of the sphere. Nor does it matter how you gauge and try him. A character is like an acrostic or Alexandrian stanza;—read it forward, backward, or across, it still spells the same thing. In this pleasing, contrite wood-life which God allows me, let me record day by day my honest thought without prospect or retrospect, and, I cannot doubt, it will be found symmetrical, though I mean it not, and see it not. My book should smell of pines and resound with the hum of insects. The swallow over my window should interweave that thread or straw he carries in his bill into my web also. We pass for what we are. Character teaches above our wills. Men imagine that they communicate their virtue or vice only by overt actions, and do not see that virtue or vice emit a breath every moment.

There will be an agreement in whatever variety of actions, so they be each honest and natural in their hour. For of one will, the actions will be harmonious, however unlike they seem. These varieties are lost sight of at a little distance, at a little height of thought. One tendency unites them all. The voyage of the best ship is a zigzag line of a hundred tacks. See the line from a sufficient distance, and it straightens itself to the average tendency. Your genuine action will explain itself, and will explain your other genuine actions. Your conformity explains nothing. Act singly, and what you have already done singly will justify you now. Greatness appeals to the future. If I can be firm enough to-day to do right, and scorn eyes, I must have done so much right before as to defend me now. Be it how it will, do right now. Always scorn appearances, and you always may. The force of character is cumulative. All the foregone days of virtue work their health into this. What makes the majesty of the heroes of the senate and the field, which so fills the imagination? The consciousness of a train of great days and victories behind. They shed an united light on the advancing actor. He is attended as by a visible escort of angels. That is it which throws thunder into Chatham's voice, and dignity into Washington's port, and America into Adams's eye. Honor is venerable to us because it is no ephemeris. It is always ancient virtue. We worship it to-day because it is not of to-day. We love it and pay it homage, because it is not a trap for our love and homage, but is self-dependent, self-derived, and therefore of an old immaculate pedigree, even if shown in a young person.

I hope in these days we have heard the last of conformity and consistency. Let the words be gazetted and ridiculous henceforward. Instead of the gong for dinner, let us hear a whistle from the Spartan fife. Let us never bow and apologize more. A great man is coming to eat at my house. I do not wish to please him; I wish that he should wish to please me. I will stand here for humanity, and though I would make it kind, I would make it true. Let us affront and reprimand the smooth mediocrity and squalid contentment of the times, and hurl in the face of custom, and trade, and office, the fact which is the upshot of all history, that there is a great responsible Thinker and Actor working wherever a man works; that a true man belongs to no other time or place, but is the centre of things. Where he is, there is nature. He measures you, and all men, and all events. Ordinarily, every body in society reminds us of somewhat else, or of some other person. Character, reality, reminds you of nothing else; it takes place of the whole creation. The man must be so much, that he must make all circumstances indifferent. Every true man is a cause, a country, and an age; requires infinite spaces and numbers and time fully to accomplish his design;—and posterity seem to follow his steps as a train of clients. A man Caesar is born, and for ages after we have a Roman Empire. Christ is born, and millions of minds so grow and cleave to his genius, that he is confounded with virtue and the possible of man. An institution is the lengthened shadow of one man; as, Monachism, of the Hermit Antony; the Reformation, of Luther; Quakerism, of Fox; Methodism, of Wesley; Abolition, of Clarkson. Scipio, Milton called "the height of Rome";

and all history resolves itself very easily into the biography of a few stout and earnest persons.

Let a man then know his worth, and keep things under his feet. Let him not peep or steal, or skulk up and down with the air of a charity-boy, a bastard, or an interloper, in the world which exists for him. But the man in the street, finding no worth in himself which corresponds to the force which built a tower or sculptured a marble god, feels poor when he looks on these. To him a palace, a statue, or a costly book have an alien and forbidding air, much like a gay equipage, and seem to say like that, 'Who are you, sir?' Yet they all are his, suitors for his notice, petitioners to his faculties that they will come out and take possession. The picture waits for my verdict: it is not to command me, but I am to settle its claims to praise. That popular fable of the sot who was picked up dead drunk in the street, carried to the duke's house, washed and dressed and laid in the duke's bed, and, on his waking, treated with all obsequious ceremony like the duke, and assured that he had been insane, owes its popularity to the fact, that it symbolizes so well the state of man, who is in the world a sort of sot, but now and then wakes up, exercises his reason, and finds himself a true prince.

Our reading is mendicant and sycophantic. In history, our imagination plays us false. Kingdom and lordship, power and estate, are a gaudier vocabulary than private John and Edward in a small house and common day's work; but the things of life are the same to both; the sum total of both is the same. Why all this deference to Alfred, and Scanderbeg, and Gustavus? Suppose they were virtuous; did they wear out virtue? As great a stake depends on your private act to-day, as followed their public and renowned steps. When private men shall act with original views, the lustre will be transferred from the actions of kings to those of gentlemen.

The world has been instructed by its kings, who have so magnetized the eyes of nations. It has been taught by this colossal symbol the mutual reverence that is due from man to man. The joyful loyalty with which men have everywhere suffered the king, the noble, or the great proprietor to walk among them by a law of his own, make his own scale of men and things, and reverse theirs, pay for benefits not with money but with honor, and represent the law in his person, was the hieroglyphic by which they obscurely signified their consciousness of their own right and comeliness, the right of every man.

The magnetism which all original action exerts is explained when we inquire the reason of self-trust. Who is the Trustee? What is the aboriginal Self, on which a universal reliance may be grounded? What is the nature and power of that science-baffling star, without parallax, without calculable elements, which shoots a ray of beauty even into trivial and impure actions, if the least mark of independence appear? The inquiry leads us to that source, at once the essence of genius, of virtue, and of life, which we call Spontaneity or Instinct. We denote this primary wisdom as Intuition, whilst all later teachings are tuitions. In that deep force, the last fact behind which analysis cannot go, all things find their common origin. For, the sense of being which in calm hours rises, we know not how, in the soul, is not diverse from things, from space, from light, from time, from man, but one with them, and proceeds obviously from the same source whence their life and being also proceed. We first share the life by which things exist, and afterwards see them as appearances in nature, and forget that we have shared their cause. Here is the fountain of action and of thought. Here are the lungs of that inspiration which giveth man wisdom, and which cannot be denied without impiety and atheism. We lie in the lap of immense intelligence, which makes us receivers of its truth and organs of its activity. When we discern justice, when we discern truth, we do nothing of ourselves, but allow a passage to its beams. If we ask whence this comes, if we seek to pry into the soul that causes, all philosophy is at fault. Its presence or its absence is all we can affirm. Every man discriminates between the voluntary acts of his mind, and his involuntary perceptions, and knows that to his involuntary perceptions a perfect faith is due. He may err in the expression of them, but he knows that these things are so, like day and night, not to be disputed. My wilful actions and acquisitions are but roving;—the idlest reverie, the faintest native emotion, command my curiosity and respect. Thoughtless people contradict as readily the statement of perceptions as of opinions, or rather much more readily; for, they do not distinguish between perception and notion. They fancy that I choose to see this or that thing. But perception is not whimsical, but fatal. If I see a trait, my children will see it after me, and in course of time, all mankind,—although it may chance that no one has seen it before me. For my perception of it is as much a fact as the sun.

The relations of the soul to the divine spirit are so pure, that it is profane to seek to interpose helps. It must be that when God speaketh he should communicate, not one thing, but all things; should fill the world with his voice; should scatter forth light, nature, time, souls, from the centre of the present thought; and new date and new create the whole. Whenever a mind is simple, and receives a divine wisdom, old things pass away,—means, teachers, texts, temples fall; it lives now, and absorbs past and future into the present hour. All things are made sacred by relation to it,—one as much as another. All things are dissolved to their centre by their cause, and, in the universal miracle, petty and particular miracles disappear. If, therefore, a man claims to know and speak of God, and carries you backward to the phraseology of some old mouldered nation in another country, in another world, believe him not. Is the acorn better than the oak which is its fulness and completion? Is the parent better than the child into whom he has cast his ripened being? Whence, then, this worship of the past? The centuries are conspirators against the sanity and authority of the soul. Time and space are but physiological colors which the eye makes, but the soul is light; where it is, is day; where it was, is night; and history is an impertinence and an injury, if it be any thing more than a cheerful apologue or parable of my being and becoming.

Man is timid and apologetic; he is no longer upright; he dares not say 'I think,' 'I am,' but quotes some saint or sage. He is ashamed before the blade of grass or the blowing rose. These roses under my window make no reference to former roses or to better ones; they are for what they are; they exist with God to-day. There is no time to them. There is simply the rose; it is perfect in every moment of its existence. Before a leaf-bud has burst, its whole life acts; in the full-blown flower there is no more; in the leafless root there is no less. Its nature is satisfied, and it satisfies nature, in all moments alike. But man postpones or remembers; he does not live in the present, but with reverted eye laments the past, or, heedless of the riches that surround him, stands on tiptoe to foresee the future. He cannot be happy and strong until he too lives with nature in the present, above time.

This should be plain enough. Yet see what strong intellects dare not yet hear God himself, unless he speak the phraseology of I know not what David, or Jeremiah, or Paul. We shall not always set so great a price on a few texts, on a few lives. We are like children who repeat by rote the sentences of grandames and tutors, and, as they grow older, of the men of talents and character they chance to see,—painfully recollecting the exact words they spoke; afterwards, when they come into the point of view which those had who uttered these sayings, they understand them, and are willing to let the words go; for, at any time, they can use words as good when occasion comes. If we live truly, we shall see truly. It is as easy for the strong man to be strong, as it is for the weak to be weak. When we have new perception, we shall gladly disburden the memory of its hoarded treasures as old rubbish. When a man lives with God, his voice shall be as sweet as the murmur of the brook and the rustle of the corn.

And now at last the highest truth on this subject remains unsaid; probably cannot be said; for all that we say is the far-off remembering of the intuition. That thought, by what I can now nearest approach to say it, is this. When good is near you, when you have life in yourself, it is not by any known or accustomed way; you shall not discern the footprints of any other; you shall not see the face of man; you shall not hear any name;—the way, the thought, the good, shall be wholly strange and new. It shall exclude example and experience. You take the way from man, not to man. All persons that ever existed are its forgotten ministers. Fear and hope are alike beneath it. There is somewhat low even in hope. In the hour of vision, there is nothing that can be called gratitude, nor properly joy. The soul raised over passion beholds identity and eternal causation, perceives the self-existence of Truth and Right, and calms itself with knowing that all things go well. Vast spaces of nature, the Atlantic Ocean, the South Sea,—long intervals of time, years, centuries,—are of no account. This which I think and feel underlay every former state of life and circumstances, as it does underlie my present, and what is called life, and what is called death.

Life only avails, not the having lived. Power ceases in the instant of repose; it resides in the moment of transition from a past to a new state, in the shooting of the gulf, in the darting to an aim. This one fact the world hates, that the soul *becomes*; for that for ever degrades the past, turns all riches to poverty, all reputation to a shame, confounds the saint with the rogue, shoves Jesus and Judas equally aside. Why, then, do we prate of self-reliance? Inasmuch as the soul is present, there will be power not confident but agent. To talk of reliance is a poor external way of speaking. Speak rather of that which relies, because it works and is. Who has more obedience than I masters me, though he should not raise his finger. Round him I must revolve by the gravitation of spirits. We fancy it rhetoric, when we speak of eminent virtue. We do not yet see that virtue is Height, and that a man or a company of men, plastic and permeable to principles, by the law of nature must overpower and ride all cities, nations, kings, rich men, poets, who are not.

This is the ultimate fact which we so quickly reach on this, as on every topic, the resolution of all into the ever-blessed ONE. Self-existence is the attribute of the Supreme Cause, and it constitutes the measure of good by the degree in which it enters into all lower forms. All things real are so by so much virtue as they contain. Commerce, husbandry, hunting, whaling, war, eloquence, personal weight, are somewhat, and engage my respect as examples of its presence and impure action. I see the same law working in nature for conservation and growth. Power is in nature the essential measure of right. Nature suffers nothing to remain in her kingdoms which cannot help itself. The genesis and maturation of a planet, its poise and orbit, the bended tree recovering itself from the strong wind, the vital resources of every animal and vegetable, are demonstrations of the self-sufficing, and therefore self-relying soul.

Thus all concentrates: let us not rove; let us sit at home with the cause. Let us stun and astonish the intruding rabble of men and books and institutions, by a simple declaration of the divine fact. Bid the invaders take the shoes from off their feet, for God is here within. Let our simplicity judge them, and our docility to our own law demonstrate the poverty of nature and fortune beside our native riches.

But now we are a mob. Man does not stand in awe of man, nor is his genius admonished to stay at home, to put itself in communication with the internal ocean, but it goes abroad to beg a cup of water of the urns of other men. We must go alone. I like the silent church before the service begins, better than any preaching. How far off, how cool, how chaste the persons look, begirt each one with a precinct or sanctuary! So let us always sit. Why should we assume the faults of our friend, or wife, or father, or child, because they sit around our hearth, or are said to have the same blood? All men have my blood, and I have all men's. Not for that will I adopt their petulance or folly, even to the extent of being ashamed of it. But your isolation must not be mechanical, but spiritual, that is, must be eleva-

tion. At times the whole world seems to be in conspiracy to importune you with emphatic trifles. Friend, client, child, sickness, fear,
want, charity, all knock at once at thy closet door, and say,—'Come
out unto us.' But keep thy state; come not into their confusion. The
power men possess to annoy me, I give them by a weak curiosity. No
man can come near me but through my act. "What we love that we
have, but by desire we bereave ourselves of the love."

If we cannot at once rise to the sanctities of obedience and faith,
let us at least resist our temptations; let us enter into the state of war,
and wake Thor and Woden, courage and constancy, in our Saxon
breasts. This is to be done in our smooth times by speaking the truth.
Check this lying hospitality and lying affection. Live no longer to the
expectation of these deceived and deceiving people with whom we
converse. Say to them, O father, O mother, O wife, O brother, O
friend, I have lived with you after appearances hitherto. Henceforward
I am the truth's. Be it known unto you that henceforward I obey no
law less than the eternal law. I will have no covenants but proximities.
I shall endeavour to nourish my parents, to support my family, to be
the chaste husband of one wife,—but these relations I must fill after a
new and unprecedented way. I appeal from your customs. I must be
myself. I cannot break myself any longer for you, or you. If you can
love me for what I am, we shall be the happier. If you cannot, I will
still seek to deserve that you should. I will not hide my tastes or aver-
sions. I will so trust that what is deep is holy, that I will do strongly
before the sun and moon whatever inly rejoices me, and the heart
appoints. If you are noble, I will love you; if you are not, I will not
hurt you and myself by hypocritical attentions. If you are true, but
not in the same truth with me, cleave to your companions; I will seek
my own. I do this not selfishly, but humbly and truly. It is alike your
interest, and mine, and all men's, however long we have dwelt in lies,
to live in truth. Does this sound harsh to-day? You will soon love
what is dictated by your nature as well as mine, and, if we follow the

truth, it will bring us out safe at last.—But so you may give these friends pain. Yes, but I cannot sell my liberty and my power, to save their sensibility. Besides, all persons have their moments of reason, when they look out into the region of absolute truth; then will they justify me, and do the same thing.

The populace think that your rejection of popular standards is a rejection of all standard, and mere antinomianism; and the bold sensualist will use the name of philosophy to gild his crimes. But the law of consciousness abides. There are two confessionals, in one or the other of which we must be shriven. You may fulfil your round of duties by clearing yourself in the direct, or in the *reflex* way. Consider whether you have satisfied your relations to father, mother, cousin, neighbour, town, cat, and dog; whether any of these can upbraid you. But I may also neglect this reflex standard, and absolve me to myself. I have my own stern claims and perfect circle. It denies the name of duty to many offices that are called duties. But if I can discharge its debts, it enables me to dispense with the popular code. If any one imagines that this law is lax, let him keep its commandment one day.

And truly it demands something godlike in him who has cast off the common motives of humanity, and has ventured to trust himself for a taskmaster. High be his heart, faithful his will, clear his sight, that he may in good earnest be doctrine, society, law, to himself, that a simple purpose may be to him as strong as iron necessity is to others!

If any man consider the present aspects of what is called by distinction *society*, he will see the need of these ethics. The sinew and heart of man seem to be drawn out, and we are become timorous, desponding whimperers. We are afraid of truth, afraid of fortune, afraid of death, and afraid of each other. Our age yields no great and perfect persons. We want men and women who shall renovate life and our social state, but we see that most natures are insolvent, cannot satisfy their own wants, have an ambition out of all proportion to their practical force, and do lean and beg day and night continually.

Our housekeeping is mendicant, our arts, our occupations, our marriages, our religion, we have not chosen, but society has chosen for us. We are parlour soldiers. We shun the rugged battle of fate, where strength is born.

If our young men miscarry in their first enterprises, they lose all heart. If the young merchant fails, men say he is *ruined*. If the finest genius studies at one of our colleges, and is not installed in an office within one year afterwards in the cities or suburbs of Boston or New York, it seems to his friends and to himself that he is right in being disheartened, and in complaining the rest of his life. A sturdy lad from New Hampshire or Vermont, who in turn tries all the professions, who *teams it, farms it, peddles*, keeps a school, preaches, edits a newspaper, goes to Congress, buys a township, and so forth, in successive years, and always, like a cat, falls on his feet, is worth a hundred of these city dolls. He walks abreast with his days, and feels no shame in not 'studying a profession,' for he does not postpone his life, but lives already. He has not one chance, but a hundred chances. Let a Stoic open the resources of man, and tell men they are not leaning willows, but can and must detach themselves; that with the exercise of self-trust, new powers shall appear; that a man is the word made flesh, born to shed healing to the nations, that he should be ashamed of our compassion, and that the moment he acts from himself, tossing the laws, the books, idolatries, and customs out of the window, we pity him no more, but thank and revere him,—and that teacher shall restore the life of man to splendor, and make his name dear to all history.

It is easy to see that a greater self-reliance must work a revolution in all the offices and relations of men; in their religion; in their education; in their pursuits; their modes of living; their association; in their property; in their speculative views.

1. In what prayers do men allow themselves! That which they call a holy office is not so much as brave and manly. Prayer looks abroad and asks for some foreign addition to come through some foreign

virtue, and loses itself in endless mazes of natural and supernatural, and mediatorial and miraculous. Prayer that craves a particular commodity,—any thing less than all good,—is vicious. Prayer is the contemplation of the facts of life from the highest point of view. It is the soliloquy of a beholding and jubilant soul. It is the spirit of God pronouncing his works good. But prayer as a means to effect a private end is meanness and theft. It supposes dualism and not unity in nature and consciousness. As soon as the man is at one with God, he will not beg. He will then see prayer in all action. The prayer of the farmer kneeling in his field to weed it, the prayer of the rower kneeling with the stroke of his oar, are true prayers heard throughout nature, though for cheap ends. Caratach, in Fletcher's Bonduca, when admonished to inquire the mind of the god Audate, replies,—

> *"His hidden meaning lies in our endeavours;*
>   *Our valours are our best gods."*

Another sort of false prayers are our regrets. Discontent is the want of self-reliance: it is infirmity of will. Regret calamities, if you can thereby help the sufferer; if not, attend your own work, and already the evil begins to be repaired. Our sympathy is just as base. We come to them who weep foolishly, and sit down and cry for company, instead of imparting to them truth and health in rough electric shocks, putting them once more in communication with their own reason. The secret of fortune is joy in our hands. Welcome evermore to gods and men is the self-helping man. For him all doors are flung wide: him all tongues greet, all honors crown, all eyes follow with desire. Our love goes out to him and embraces him, because he did not need it. We solicitously and apologetically caress and celebrate him, because he held on his way and scorned our disapprobation. The gods love him because men hated him. "To the persevering mortal," said Zoroaster, "the blessed Immortals are swift."

As men's prayers are a disease of the will, so are their creeds a disease of the intellect. They say with those foolish Israelites, 'Let not God speak to us, lest we die. Speak thou, speak any man with us, and we will obey.' Everywhere I am hindered of meeting God in my brother, because he has shut his own temple doors, and recites fables merely of his brother's, or his brother's brother's God. Every new mind is a new classification. If it prove a mind of uncommon activity and power, a Locke, a Lavoisier, a Hutton, a Bentham, a Fourier, it imposes its classification on other men, and lo! a new system. In proportion to the depth of the thought, and so to the number of the objects it touches and brings within reach of the pupil, is his complacency. But chiefly is this apparent in creeds and churches, which are also classifications of some powerful mind acting on the elemental thought of duty, and man's relation to the Highest. Such is Calvinism, Quakerism, Swedenborgism. The pupil takes the same delight in subordinating every thing to the new terminology, as a girl who has just learned botany in seeing a new earth and new seasons thereby. It will happen for a time, that the pupil will find his intellectual power has grown by the study of his master's mind. But in all unbalanced minds, the classification is idolized, passes for the end, and not for a speedily exhaustible means, so that the walls of the system blend to their eye in the remote horizon with the walls of the universe; the luminaries of heaven seem to them hung on the arch their master built. They cannot imagine how you aliens have any right to see,—how you can see; 'It must be somehow that you stole the light from us.' They do not yet perceive, that light, unsystematic, indomitable, will break into any cabin, even into theirs. Let them chirp awhile and call it their own. If they are honest and do well, presently their neat new pinfold will be too strait and low, will crack, will lean, will rot and vanish, and the immortal light, all young and joyful, million-orbed, million-colored, will beam over the universe as on the first morning.

2. It is for want of self-culture that the superstition of Travelling, whose idols are Italy, England, Egypt, retains its fascination for all educated Americans. They who made England, Italy, or Greece venerable in the imagination did so by sticking fast where they were, like an axis of the earth. In manly hours, we feel that duty is our place. The soul is no traveller; the wise man stays at home, and when his necessities, his duties, on any occasion call him from his house, or into foreign lands, he is at home still, and shall make men sensible by the expression of his countenance, that he goes the missionary of wisdom and virtue, and visits cities and men like a sovereign, and not like an interloper or a valet.

I have no churlish objection to the circumnavigation of the globe, for the purposes of art, of study, and benevolence, so that the man is first domesticated, or does not go abroad with the hope of finding somewhat greater than he knows. He who travels to be amused, or to get somewhat which he does not carry, travels away from himself, and grows old even in youth among old things. In Thebes, in Palmyra, his will and mind have become old and dilapidated as they. He carries ruins to ruins.

Travelling is a fool's paradise. Our first journeys discover to us the indifference of places. At home I dream that at Naples, at Rome, I can be intoxicated with beauty, and lose my sadness. I pack my trunk, embrace my friends, embark on the sea, and at last wake up in Naples, and there beside me is the stern fact, the sad self, unrelenting, identical, that I fled from. I seek the Vatican, and the palaces. I affect to be intoxicated with sights and suggestions, but I am not intoxicated. My giant goes with me wherever I go.

3. But the rage of travelling is a symptom of a deeper unsoundness affecting the whole intellectual action. The intellect is vagabond, and our system of education fosters restlessness. Our minds travel when our bodies are forced to stay at home. We imitate; and what is imitation but the travelling of the mind? Our houses are built with foreign taste; our

shelves are garnished with foreign ornaments; our opinions, our tastes, our faculties, lean, and follow the Past and the Distant. The soul created the arts wherever they have flourished. It was in his own mind that the artist sought his model. It was an application of his own thought to the thing to be done and the conditions to be observed. And why need we copy the Doric or the Gothic model? Beauty, convenience, grandeur of thought, and quaint expression are as near to us as to any, and if the American artist will study with hope and love the precise thing to be done by him, considering the climate, the soil, the length of the day, the wants of the people, the habit and form of the government, he will create a house in which all these will find themselves fitted, and taste and sentiment will be satisfied also.

Insist on yourself; never imitate. Your own gift you can present every moment with the cumulative force of a whole life's cultivation; but of the adopted talent of another, you have only an extemporaneous, half possession. That which each can do best, none but his Maker can teach him. No man yet knows what it is, nor can, till that person has exhibited it. Where is the master who could have taught Shakespeare? Where is the master who could have instructed Franklin, or Washington, or Bacon, or Newton? Every great man is a unique. The Scipionism of Scipio is precisely that part he could not borrow. Shakespeare will never be made by the study of Shakespeare. Do that which is assigned you, and you cannot hope too much or dare too much. There is at this moment for you an utterance brave and grand as that of the colossal chisel of Phidias, or trowel of the Egyptians, or the pen of Moses, or Dante, but different from all these. Not possibly will the soul all rich, all eloquent, with thousand-cloven tongue, deign to repeat itself; but if you can hear what these patriarchs say, surely you can reply to them in the same pitch of voice; for the ear and the tongue are two organs of one nature. Abide in the simple and noble regions of thy life, obey thy heart, and thou shalt reproduce the Foreworld again.

4. As our Religion, our Education, our Art look abroad, so does our spirit of society. All men plume themselves on the improvement of society, and no man improves.

Society never advances. It recedes as fast on one side as it gains on the other. It undergoes continual changes; it is barbarous, it is civilized, it is christianized, it is rich, it is scientific; but this change is not amelioration. For every thing that is given, something is taken. Society acquires new arts, and loses old instincts. What a contrast between the well-clad, reading, writing, thinking American, with a watch, a pencil, and a bill of exchange in his pocket, and the naked New Zealander, whose property is a club, a spear, a mat, and an undivided twentieth of a shed to sleep under! But compare the health of the two men, and you shall see that the white man has lost his aboriginal strength. If the traveller tell us truly, strike the savage with a broad axe, and in a day or two the flesh shall unite and heal as if you struck the blow into soft pitch, and the same blow shall send the white to his grave.

The civilized man has built a coach, but has lost the use of his feet. He is supported on crutches, but lacks so much support of muscle. He has a fine Geneva watch, but he fails of the skill to tell the hour by the sun. A Greenwich nautical almanac he has, and so being sure of the information when he wants it, the man in the street does not know a star in the sky. The solstice he does not observe; the equinox he knows as little; and the whole bright calendar of the year is without a dial in his mind. His note-books impair his memory; his libraries overload his wit; the insurance-office increases the number of accidents; and it may be a question whether machinery does not encumber; whether we have not lost by refinement some energy, by a Christianity entrenched in establishments and forms, some vigor of wild virtue. For every Stoic was a Stoic; but in Christendom where is the Christian?

There is no more deviation in the moral standard than in the standard of height or bulk. No greater men are now than ever were.

A singular equality may be observed between the great men of the first and of the last ages; nor can all the science, art, religion, and philosophy of the nineteenth century avail to educate greater men than Plutarch's heroes, three or four and twenty centuries ago. Not in time is the race progressive. Phocion, Socrates, Anaxagoras, Diogenes, are great men, but they leave no class. He who is really of their class will not be called by their name, but will be his own man, and, in his turn, the founder of a sect. The arts and inventions of each period are only its costume, and do not invigorate men. The harm of the improved machinery may compensate its good. Hudson and Behring accomplished so much in their fishing-boats, as to astonish Parry and Franklin, whose equipment exhausted the resources of science and art. Galileo, with an opera-glass, discovered a more splendid series of celestial phenomena than any one since. Columbus found the New World in an undecked boat. It is curious to see the periodical disuse and perishing of means and machinery, which were introduced with loud laudation a few years or centuries before. The great genius returns to essential man. We reckoned the improvements of the art of war among the triumphs of science, and yet Napoleon conquered Europe by the bivouac, which consisted of falling back on naked valor, and disencumbering it of all aids. The Emperor held it impossible to make a perfect army, says Las Casas, "without abolishing our arms, magazines, commissaries, and carriages, until, in imitation of the Roman custom, the soldier should receive his supply of corn, grind it in his hand-mill, and bake his bread himself."

Society is a wave. The wave moves onward, but the water of which it is composed does not. The same particle does not rise from the valley to the ridge. Its unity is only phenomenal. The persons who make up a nation to-day, next year die, and their experience with them.

And so the reliance on Property, including the reliance on governments which protect it, is the want of self-reliance. Men have looked away from themselves and at things so long, that they have come to esteem the religious, learned, and civil institutions as guards of property, and they deprecate assaults on these, because they feel them to be assaults on property. They measure their esteem of each other by what each has, and not by what each is. But a cultivated man becomes ashamed of his property, out of new respect for his nature. Especially he hates what he has, if he see that it is accidental,—came to him by inheritance, or gift, or crime; then he feels that it is not having; it does not belong to him, has no root in him, and merely lies there, because no revolution or no robber takes it away. But that which a man is does always by necessity acquire, and what the man acquires is living property, which does not wait the beck of rulers, or mobs, or revolutions, or fire, or storm, or bankruptcies, but perpetually renews itself wherever the man breathes. "Thy lot or portion of life," said the Caliph Ali, "is seeking after thee; therefore be at rest from seeking after it." Our dependence on these foreign goods leads us to our slavish respect for numbers. The political parties meet in numerous conventions; the greater the concourse, and with each new uproar of announcement, The delegation from Essex! The Democrats from New Hampshire! The Whigs of Maine! the young patriot feels himself stronger than before by a new thousand of eyes and arms. In like manner the reformers summon conventions, and vote and resolve in multitude. Not so, O friends! will the God deign to enter and inhabit you, but by a method precisely the reverse. It is only as a man puts off all foreign support, and stands alone, that I see him to be strong and to prevail. He is weaker by every recruit to his banner. Is not a man better than a town? Ask nothing of men, and in the endless mutation, thou only firm column must presently appear the upholder of all that surrounds thee. He who knows that power is inborn, that he is weak because he has looked for good out of him and elsewhere, and so perceiving, throws himself unhesitatingly on his thought, instantly rights himself, stands in the erect position, commands his limbs, works miracles; just as a man who stands on his feet is stronger than a man who stands on his head.

So use all that is called Fortune. Most men gamble with her, and gain all, and lose all, as her wheel rolls. But do thou leave as unlawful these winnings, and deal with Cause and Effect, the chancellors of God. In the Will work and acquire, and thou hast chained the wheel of Chance, and shalt sit hereafter out of fear from her rotations. A political victory, a rise of rents, the recovery of your sick, or the return of your absent friend, or some other favorable event, raises your spirits, and you think good days are preparing for you. Do not believe it. Nothing can bring you peace but yourself. Nothing can bring you peace but the triumph of principles.